INSIDE The CHINESE MIND

A GUIDE ON HOW THE CHINESE THINK

INSIDE THE CHINESE MIND

A GUIDE ON HOW THE CHINESE THINK

Geoff Baker
Helen Zhang

Andover • Melbourne • Mexico City • Stamford, CT • Toronto • Hong Kong • New Delhi • Seoul • Singapore • Tokyo

**Inside the Chinese Mind
A Guide on How the
Chinese Think**
Geoff Baker
Helen Zhang

Publishing Director:
Paul K. H. Tan

Editorial Manager:
Yang Liping

Development Editor (Media):
Tanmayee Bhatwadekar

Associate Development Editor:
Doris Wai

Senior Regional Director:
Janet Lim

Product Manager:
Tan Lee Hong

Production Manager:
Pauline Lim

Production Executive:
Cindy Chai

Copy Editor:
Jane Lael

Cover Designer:
Ong Lay Keng

Compositor:
diacriTech, Inc

© 2012 Cengage Learning Asia Pte Ltd

ALL RIGHTS RESERVED. No part of this work covered by the copyright herein may be reproduced, transmitted, stored or used in any form or by any means graphic, electronic, or mechanical, including but not limited to photocopying, recording, scanning, digitalizing, taping, Web distribution, information networks, or information storage and retrieval systems, without the prior written permission of the publisher.

For product information and technology assistance, contact us at **Cengage Learning Asia Customer Support, 65-6410-1200**

For permission to use material from this text or product, submit all requests online at
www.cengageasia.com/permissions
Further permissions questions can be emailed to
asia.permissionrequest@cengage.com

ISBN-13: 978-981-4392-77-8
ISBN-10: 981-4392-77-4

Cengage Learning Asia Pte Ltd
151 Lorong Chuan
#02-08 New Tech Park
Singapore 556741

Cengage Learning is a leading provider of customized learning solutions with office locations around the globe, including Andover, Melbourne, Mexico City, Stamford (CT), Toronto, Hong Kong, New Delhi, Seoul, Singapore, and Tokyo. Locate your local office at **www.cengage.com/global**

Cengage Learning products are represented in Canada by Nelson Education, Ltd.

For product information, visit **www.cengageasia.com**

Printed in Singapore
1 2 3 4 5 15 14 13 12

Contents

Acknowledgements	ix
Chapter 1 Introduction	1
Global TechCo's Long March	1
The Founder's Journey into China	2
Alarm Bells Chiming	2
The Scene is Set	4
Journey into China and the Chinese Mind	4
Chinese Secrets Revealed	5
This Book is for…	5
An Insider's View	6
Who Are the Authors?	6
Structure of the Book	7
Find a Brilliant Horse	8
Chapter 2 Chinese Thinking: The Five Core Elements	9
Core Element No. 1: Language that Shapes the Mind	11
Core Element No. 2: The Law of Yin (阴) and Yang (阳)—The Unity of Opposites	17
Core Element No. 3: Chinese Connectedness—"Born Equal" versus "Born Connected"	19
Core Element No. 4: Midstream Living	22
Core Element No. 5: Face 面子 Mianzi—More Important than Life Itself	25
A Glimpse of History	27
Conclusion	28

Chapter 3   The Emerging Superpower — 29

100 Years of Humiliation — 30
History in the Making — 31
What is Happiness in China? — 33
China Insights — 35
Conclusion — 49
A Grain of Salt — 50

Chapter 4   Chinese Leadership — 51

Different Paths, Different Leaders — 52
Different Generations of Chinese Leaders — 54
Women Who Shape China — 58
Leaders and Decision Makers—The Chinese Definition — 60
Leadership—The Chinese Definition — 61
The SOE Syndrome — 62
Clashing Leadership Styles — 63
SOEs and the Ultimate Leader — 64
Chinese Leadership Styles — 65
The Impact of Confucianism — 69
Conclusion — 72

Chapter 5   Work Ethics — 73

Historical Context — 74
Cultural Context — 76
Chinese Generation Y — 82
Chinese Work Ethics — 83
Conclusion — 88

Chapter 6   How the Chinese Communicate — 89

What We Say about Each Other — 90
Important Chinese Communication Terms — 91
Seven Reasons The Chinese Communicate Differently — 95
Implied Rules That The Chinese Follow — 102
Conclusion — 108

Chapter 7 Chinese Relationships — 111

Chinese "Circles of Influence" — 113
Are the Chinese Really so Different? — 126
The Arrival of an Extra-Terrestrial (E.T.) — 127
Conclusion — 128

Chapter 8 Small Things — 129

Can Foreigners Be "Real" Friends with the Local Chinese? — 129
Food is the Sky — 131
The Importance of Business Banquets — 132
Big Things for the Chinese: Do Not Be Seen in a Taxi — 134
Big Things for the Chinese: Chinese Festivals — 135
Big Things for the Chinese: Appropriate Gifts — 136
When Big is Small: When Chinese Mr. Near Enough Meets the Detail Devil — 137
First Impressions Do Count — 138
When Small is Big — 139
Small Things that Annoy the Chinese — 141
Small Things that Annoy Foreigners — 142
Answer that Phone! — 143
Conclusion — 144

Chapter 9 Dealing with Conflict — 147

Historical Context — 149
Cultural Context — 150
Dispute Resolution — 156
Into the Abyss — 160
Tips from The Tale of Woe — 163
Conclusion — 163

Chapter 10 Localization and Intellectual Property — 165

Historical Context — 166
Cultural Context — 167
The Chinese View of "Give and Take" — 167

How the Chinese View Branding	168
Three-and-a-Half Chinese Localization Models	170
Paradigm Shift: From a World Factory to a World Laboratory	176
Emerging Scientific Superpower	176
Rush to Research and Development (R&D)	177
Going Global	178
How Foreign Businesses Localize	178
Three Localization Approaches	179
Seven Ways to Protect IP	179
Conclusion	182
Chapter 11 Conclusion	**183**
Index	**185**

Acknowledgements

"A single conversation with a wise man is better than ten years of study"
Anonymous—Chinese Proverb

Two thousand years ago, a musician called Boya studied the principles of guqin (one of the world's most ancient musical instruments) under a renowned teacher. After years of learning, however, he found himself still inferior to his teacher and felt deeply dissatisfied with himself. One day, the teacher told him, "I will take you to meet my own teacher."

The teacher took him to a remote island, and they sat down on the peak of a small hill overlooking the island and the ocean. They sat in silence for a long time. Then the teacher stood up and said to Boya, "You stay here and wait; I will go find the Master."

Boya stayed and waited. Three days passed and he was still waiting and naturally, growing somewhat anxious. Then as if for the first time, he heard the sound of the waves, the wind racing across the sand, and sea birds singing.

"A-ha!" suddenly Boya understood. He took his guqin, put it on his knees, and began to play. The sound came out of his fingers, and blended with the waves, the wind, and the singing of the birds into a most beautiful song.

Like Boya, we have been students eager to learn about China. We worked passionately, discussed endlessly, living and breathing through the chapters, sections, paragraphs, and words. Writing this book has made us realize how much we don't know and how much we have learned (and are still learning). On this most fascinating journey, we have been blessed to have met many great teachers, without whose help and guidance this book would not be what it is today.

Madame Wei Wu, our most admired friend who first connected us with our publisher; Doris and John whose guidance and mentoring have been invaluable; Min Yang, we have learned so much from you; Anna and Arthur, our over qualified consulting editors—how could we ever repay your generosity for giving up precious time under the Tuscan sun to sprinkle your magic through the chapters; Dr Yanli Gao thank you for the pointers and discussions; Dr. Xisu Wang, we appreciate your knowledge and thought-provoking remarks on Chinese culture and philosophy.

We are also empowered by all the brilliant contemporary Chinese business and thought leaders. Thank you Aji for all your frank and insightful remarks; Jerry, your encouragement has carried us through some tough moments; Yang, your work has been truly inspirational. Catherine and Eric—you never stop amazing us with your achievements and experience; Xiuping and Wen, we are beneficiaries of your infectious optimism and generosity; and Larry, our dear American friend, thank you for keeping our feet on the ground with your practical insights.

Our gratitude also goes to our non-Chinese colleagues, business partners, and friends around the globe for entrusting us with the privilege to work with you on various projects through the years. We are grateful to James, who has taught us so much; Professor Barrell, for being such a wonderful teacher and friend of China; Professor Hampden-Turner, for his sharp intellect, vast knowledge on cross-culture, entrepreneurship, and creativity; Larry, from London, for his thorough professionalism and global insight. Mr. Saint-Marc, your presence is greatly missed; Simone, we look forward to our next face-to-face discussion in Germany; Henk, it was great fun working with you in the Netherlands.

All writers know that each and every book is only made possible through the endorsement, hard work, and support of the publisher. Thanks to Ms. Caroline Ma, China Manager—we are fortunate to have found our book in the capable hands of Cengage Learning. We admire the leadership of Mr. Tan Tat Chu, President of Asia-Pacific and Mr. Paul Tan, Senior Regional Director for Greater China. We are grateful to Mr. Liping Yang, Editorial Manager; Ms Tanmayee Bhatwadekar, Development Editor; Copy Editor Jane Lael; and Associate Development Editor, Doris Wai.

We thank all our loved ones and friends who have tolerated us all the way through—you know who you are and we remain eternally indebted to your unconditional love.

Most importantly, we want to thank YOU, for entrusting us and accepting our invitation to embark upon the journey into the Chinese minds. May you find it equally fascinating and rewarding. Enjoy!

Helen & Geoff

Chapter 1

Introduction

In China, everything is possible, but nothing is easy
Anonymous

The quote "In China, everything is possible, but nothing is easy" captures all that is good and bad in China today. Through the story that follows, you will begin to understand why.

It began as a fairly typical and straightforward Chinese acquisition of an overseas technology company. What happened next, however, was a series of rollercoaster stranger than fiction events that highlight a number of typical pitfalls when doing business in China. We have changed the names to protect the guilty, and of course the innocent, to maintain "face" for all.

GLOBAL TECHCO'S LONG MARCH

Helen's old client Tom asked her once again to act as his China guide during an upcoming visit to China. Tom is the chief executive officer (CEO) of Global TechCo, a leading new technology company. In the past, Helen had assisted the company to assess various joint ventures and potential business partners in China.

The purpose of the trip was to visit a consortium made up of key government officials from the development zone, key investor Mr. Hu, and entrepreneur Mr. Wang, in Kunshan, a small provincial city close to Shanghai. The visit was organized by introducer/middleman, Carl, who plays a critical part in the entire saga.

Carl, a thirty-something young man from Northern China, had studied for a few years in Europe. During that time, he met and befriended the founder of Global TechCo. Carl owns a trading company that sources goods from the Kunshan region and exports them to Europe. He is passionate, highly emotional, and enjoys the finer things in life, but has little experience in joint ventures and simply none in cross-border mergers and acquisition transactions. About six months prior to Tom's visit, Carl had introduced some key people from Kunshan to the founder when he was in China for a conference. Subsequently, the Chinese formed a consortium, which then visited Global TechCo's European headquarters.

The Founder's Journey into China

While CEO Tom was busy managing the company's rapid expansion in both Europe and America, the founder had been making many trips to China, returning each time with grand promises from his new and wonderful "Chinese friends." He spoke lavishly about Carl and persuaded Tom to make Carl the company's "China Representative," and to fund his operations in Beijing in order to assist Global TechCo to establish its brand and credibility in China.

When Tom first met Carl in Europe, he asked Carl what his expectations were in terms of financial rewards. Carl said, "Nothing. I am not expecting anything, just helping friends." (Red light: this is a typical Chinese middleman statement. Instead of expressing his real motivation, Carl chose to lie about what he really wanted. When faced with a similar situation, care must be taken.)

Carl was subsequently given a company credit card for expenses incurred on behalf of Global TechCo. However, the company controller had to stop his card after three months, as Carl had withdrawn the maximum amount of cash allowed at the beginning of every month and was unable to provide details or evidence to account for it.

Tom went to China to meet the consortium before its representatives went to Europe, and witnessed Carl in operation. There was no clear agenda. Each day, they were shuffled around to factories and places, which left little time to discuss business. While there was some order in the chaos and genuine interest from the Chinese investors, it appeared that Carl had no intention of taking Tom to speak with them directly.

Alarm Bells Chiming

Tom also saw that Carl was using a Mercedes that he had "borrowed" from his Chinese friends and was paying large amounts of cash to the driver. All sorts of alarm bells went off in seasoned "China hand" Tom's head when this happened. (Red light: In China, one never pays a true friend's driver in cash. Paying in cash signifies that they are not really friends, or are stretching the truth.)

Upon returning to Europe, Tom immediately ordered a due diligence check on Carl, which reinforced his suspicions. Carl claimed that he had worked and studied at a couple of top firms and universities in China, all of which appeared fabricated.

There was more. Tom had sent a trusted advisor, a Taiwanese Chinese consultant, to accompany and guide his founder during another of his ever-mounting China visits. The consultant resigned on the second day of the trip. Carl reported that the Chinese investors found him making offensive Taiwanese remarks at the after-dinner karaoke session.

Tom discussed the situation with the consultant, who said, with anger, that he had been compromised, as Carl had privately offered to buy him off. When he refused the bribery, he was marginalized politically so that he would not be a threat to Carl. Helen was seriously concerned by this series of events.

By now, the investment structure was becoming clear. Carl was able to articulate verbally (nothing in writing yet) that the Chinese consortium was able to get some land at a cheap price (probably for nothing but that was not disclosed); then Mr Hu had a company that was very complementary to Global TechCo so they could join forces to set up a manufacturing facility in Kunshan. The local government would back this initiative with tens of millions of US dollars in grants as Global TechCo's technology was strategically important for China, meeting all appropriate investment criteria. The project would be awash in money and all parties would be rewarded handsomely.

So they went the next step. Carl took the Chinese delegation—government officials and business delegates from Kunshan—to visit the company's European head office.

After the consortium delegation went to Europe, they submitted a tentative offer via Carl, expressing their intent to acquire the entire company for a certain large amount of money (but not satisfactory to all Global TechCo shareholders).

When Tom received the offer from Carl, he asked Carl again what he wanted out of the deal. Carl said, "Nothing, I'm just trying to help out my good friend (the founder)."

Tom and the executive team took the offer seriously. They reported to the Board and communicated via Carl to the Chinese group the necessary steps to further the discussions. After that communication, however, there was no response from the Chinese investor group. Carl emailed Tom to say that he had worked so hard for the deal, that he felt terribly ill and would need to claim Euro 30,000 as compensation for his medical expenses. He claimed, "It's not about the money; it's about feelings." (Tom's comment: "I don't pay for feelings, my friend!")

Carl suddenly changed his attitude and demanded a 10 percent introduction fee for any potential investment that the company was going to receive from the Chinese consortium.

All this made Tom wonder whether the deal was for real, or just a story fabricated to support Carl's lavish lifestyle. As Tom was also obligated to give the Board of Directors his recommendation, he decided to allocate five days to get to the bottom of this proposal by visiting China.

He was also determined, with Helen's assistance, to meet and talk to the key people in the consortium to assess how genuine the offer was. Tom also knew that he had to clearly communicate to the Chinese that the founder was not the decision-maker for the deal to go ahead, even though the founder may have made some expansive and empty promises. (Back in the European office, the founder was beginning to make outlandish statements about the company's global dominance because of his great work in China, and even volunteered to head the newly structured company with a Chinese operation.)

The Scene is Set

Tom and Helen reviewed the situation carefully before visiting Kunshan. Helen suggested that she should be introduced as a translator to protect her involvement and allow her to move more freely between the parties. In so doing, she hoped Carl would not see her as a threat.

However, immediately after her appointment was confirmed, Carl rang to ascertain her involvement and background. Helen could hear the doubt and concern in his voice. Obviously, he wanted to ensure that any new Chinese player was not going to be a threat.

Helen, in character, said she was there only to translate as she had helped Tom and Global TechCo in the past. She made it clear that she was not an employee and would not be involved in any long-term plans.

If you think the various relationships and key events leading up to Tom's trip with Helen sound complex and bizarre, what followed was a chain of events that unfolded in a "very Chinese" way. Due to its intricate and complex nature, the "long march" will be studied in several related chapters, as it deserves in-depth analysis and discussion that will reveal many aspects of doing business in China.

Journey into China and the Chinese Mind

The story of Global TechCo shows that modern China does sometimes resemble "the wild wild West." What is China to you? A mysterious communist country with far too many people? A huge and expanding market for your business? A gigantic factory that produces anything and everything at low cost?

A Western friend commented after her first visit to Shanghai: "Wherever you look, there are just SO many people! My daughters are going to marry the Chinese when they grow up!" Well, that may be China's last export commodity—but have you ever wondered how China and the Chinese will impact your work and your life?

We invite you to join us on a fascinating journey to China—the second-largest economy in the world, just behind the United States. Like an enormous kaleidoscope, China presents fascinating, ever-changing pictures—the patterns often amazingly complex, chaotic, and never the same. Throughout this book we do our best to present these striking views in a way that reveals a true China.

The "hands" maneuvering this giant kaleidoscope are those of the Chinese people—who live in Beijing, Shanghai, and other big cities, and in the western areas that stretch from Lhasa to Kunming. They are the hands of decision-makers in government, and those of migrant workers. They are the hands of the old and young, men and women, from all walks of life. These people have made China what it is today. Our lens focuses on them. We take you behind the scenes, to peek inside their minds.

CHINESE SECRETS REVEALED

We invite you to consider the following questions:

- When does a Chinese "yes" mean "yes?" Or "maybe?" Or "no?"
- Do you communicate in a way that the Chinese counterpart can understand exactly what you mean?
- Do you know how to effectively network with the Chinese?
- Do you understand 面子 *mianzi* (face) like the Chinese do?
- Do you know how to effectively manage the Chinese?
- Have you heard of 山寨 *shanzhai*?
- Is the Chinese Gen Y westernizing or modernizing?
- Can you distinguish 忽悠 *hoo you* from 靠谱 cow poo—that is, Chinese "facts" or "true statements" from the "bragging" and "bullshit" used to describe over-inflated Chinese statements?

All these and more will be addressed at length.

THIS BOOK IS FOR...

Those who are intrigued by or connected to China, who want to know what and how the Chinese think, and who want to gain some fundamental understanding of why the Chinese behave in certain ways.

More specifically, it is for

- those who are interested in the future of our "global village" and how it will be shaped by the emergence of China as a world superpower;
- those who want to understand some of the underlying Chinese behaviors with the intent to make more informed decisions or take appropriate actions when dealing with the Chinese at work or socially;
- those who work with Chinese partners or manage Chinese employees; or
- those who are simply interested in China, its culture, and its people.

An Insider's View

We share insights on how to

- better appreciate and understand where the Chinese come from and why they think differently from people who have grown up in Western cultures;
- approach things with a more "Chinese" attitude and find new ways to live, work, or relate to others;
- make more Chinese friends and extend your circles of influence;
- better lead, motivate, and manage Chinese employees and relationships; and
- simply understand China and the Chinese better!

Sun Zi said, "Know yourself and your enemy, then you will never lose a battle."[1] We say, "Know the Chinese mind so you can prosper!"

Who Are the Authors?

During our many years of working and living in China, both of us—Haihua Zhang (also known as Helen) and Geoff Baker—have been fortunate to be exposed to the fascinating Chinese world, individually and jointly.

Haihua was born in mainland China. After finishing her degree at Peking University in Beijing, she lived in Australia for eight years working in both management consulting and investment banking fields before relocating back to China in 2002 as a "sea turtle," the name given to native Chinese returnees—as the word 海归 *hai gui* sounds exactly the same as 海龟 "sea turtle" in Mandarin. Haihua is a writer, business advisor on China, and the mother of our two children.

Geoff is an Australian. However, the Chinese refer to people like him as an egg—"white" outside but "yellow" inside—which is to say he is Chinese in essence. A starry-eyed Westerner, always fascinated by China, Geoff is a lawyer, investment banker, and a keen entrepreneur and businessman who has worked, invested, and lived in China since the early nineties.

Over the years, we began to compare Western and Eastern perspectives and put them into practice in our lives and business dealings. We found that certain principles apply to both, while others are deeply embedded in Chinese thinking and are totally unfamiliar to someone from the West. Furthermore, because we have different lenses (one Eastern, one Western), often we have very different perspectives.

---

[1] Sun Tzu, *On the Art of War, The Oldest Military Treatise of the World*, translated by Lionel Giles, (London 1910).

We learned that China is a vast, diverse, and multilayered country. Chinese people come from equally diverse backgrounds and support different ideas and thinking. Some see business success as a goal in life, while others pursue academic, scientific, or spiritual enlightenment.

We are privileged to have many fascinating, intelligent, and unique Chinese and Western friends and business associates. They have generously shared with us their invaluable insights, stories, and business experiences in China.

Slowly, patterns emerged from the many seemingly fragmented and unrelated materials we gathered. We are now able to better understand and appreciate what the Chinese think and why they act in different ways. The pictures made sense only when we combined our views.

This book presents the patterns we have put together through our fascinating China journey in both business and social arenas, and our discoveries of the key areas that differentiate Chinese thinking from Western, particularly when it comes to the Chinese dealing with foreigners or the Chinese conducting themselves outside China.

Writing this book has been an incredibly fulfilling experience. We "learned, un-learned, and re-learned," which enabled us to further appreciate the wonderful differences and similarities between the Chinese people and those from the West. As the well-known and widely travelled Polish journalist Ryszard Kapuściński once said, "Cultures of others serve as a mirror in which we can examine ourselves, thanks to which we understand ourselves better—for we cannot define our own identity until having confronted that of others, as a comparison."[2]

STRUCTURE OF THE BOOK

Chapters 2 and 3 put things into perspective. "Five Core Elements" elaborates on how Chinese think conceptually, culturally, and historically. "Emerging Superpower" shows how this relates and applies to current China.

The following chapters look into certain challenges or misconceptions with regard to understanding and working with the Chinese:

- **Chapter 4** examines how some Chinese view leadership and compares it to the Western concept of leadership.
- **Chapter 5** explains why and how most Chinese employees follow well-established Chinese philosophies in how they approach work.
- **Chapter 6** explores the Chinese style of communication, which is completely different from that of the Westerners.

---

[2] Ryszard, Kapuściński, *Travels with Herodotus*, Chinese version, translated by Dr. Lan Wu (Beijing: People's Literature Publishing, 2009).

- **Chapter 7** reveals key differences between the way the Chinese and Western business people form and maintain relationships.
- **Chapter 8** identifies many things that can annoy Chinese in their dealings with foreigners—and vice versa.
- **Chapter 9** explains how the law operates differently in China from that in the West, and how is it that the Chinese have a fundamentally different attitude toward dispute resolution.
- **Chapter 10** looks at efforts made and laws changed to protect intellectual property (IP) and evaluates some of the most commonly adopted IP strategies used by both international and Chinese companies.

In each chapter, we quote well-known Chinese fables and sayings, and explain how they fit into the particular context. We explore where and how such differences arise by exploring relevant cultural, social, and economic issues, illustrated with true stories.

FIND A BRILLIANT HORSE

Many centuries ago in China, there lived the famous horse-judging master Bo Le. His passion was to recognize the essential elements of a brilliant horse. He wrote the classic book *Xiang Ma Jing* (相马经) on how to help people judge such horses. He described a "brilliant horse" as "an animal with a wide forehead, bulging eyes, and round hoofs."

Inspired by this wonderful book, Bo Le's son went out one day to search for a brilliant horse. After a while, he returned, bringing with him a toad!

He proudly said, "Father, I have found a horse very similar to what you described, except that its eyes are not bulging enough and its hooves are not very round."

Master Bo Le did not know whether to laugh or to cry. He pondered for a while, then replied: "What you've done is to look for a horse according to the description only. This horse may be good at jumping, but I would not want to ride it!"

Like Master Bo Le, whose passion was to find brilliant horses, we are passionate about China and Chinese people. Our intent is to help you truly understand China and the Chinese. However, as much as we have endeavored mightily, remember that what you read are only "descriptions"—the danger of finding a toad instead of a brilliant horse still exists!

Chapter 2

Chinese Thinking: The Five Core Elements

Study the past when you want to define the future
Confucius, *Analects*

In ancient China, there were two very large mountains, Tai Hang and Wang Wu, each many thousands of feet high and hundreds of miles in circumference. A humble old man, Yu Gong, lived to the north of these. Yu's house faced the mountains and he found it very inconvenient to have to detour around them every time he travelled away from home.

He called a family meeting with his sons and wife to discuss this problem. "I'd like us to consider working together to level these mountains. We can then open up a road southward to the banks of the Han River."

All his sons agreed, but his wife was a little doubtful. "You do not have the strength to level even a small hill!" she protested. "How can you move two mountains? Besides, where are you going to dump all the earth and rocks?"

"We can dump them in the river," he said.

Then Yu Gong and his sons set out with carrying poles, digging up stones and earth, and carrying them to the sea. A neighbor saw all this activity and although a widow, she sent her son to help Yu and his family. It took them several months to make just one trip, but they kept working diligently.

A reputed wise man lived by the shore of the Han River; somewhat bemused by all their efforts, he decided to do his best to stop them.

"Enough! Please! Enough of all this folly!" the wise man cried to Yu Gong. "This is just plain stupid. You are old and weak and will not be able to remove even a fraction of these mountains. How can you dispose of so many stones and so much earth?"

Old Yu heaved a long sigh. "I thought you were a wise man! You do not even have the sense of the widow's young son. Even though I may die soon, I will leave behind my sons, they will leave behind their sons, and so on, from generation to generation. As these mountains will not grow any more, why shouldn't we be able to level them?"

In a review of The Geography of Thought by Richard Nesbitt, the *Providence Journal-Bulletin* remarks that "an understanding of the thought processes of other cultures may very well be essential to the survival of Western civilization." This is indeed true. It is now critical for the world to gain a better appreciation of what is inside the Chinese mind. How and where should one start?

Confucius (551–479 BC) said, "One must study the past to define the future." It holds true today—modern Chinese rely on the past to navigate the present and prepare for the future, a future where China will surely emerge as the next world superpower.

To gain a fundamental understanding of today's Chinese and where they are going, it is necessary to learn where they have been. Below are five of the most prevailing and relevant concepts that significantly influence how the Chinese think and behave.

Zhang Ruimin, CEO of Haier (a high-profile and much-admired Chinese CEO) attributes his success in building and managing one of the world's largest white goods manufacturing groups to the application of ancient Chinese thinking that he learned from *Lao Zi* (Taoism), *The Analects of Confucius* (the collection of sayings and teachings of Confucius), and Sun Zi's *The Art of War*.

China's culture and history date back to more than 5,000 years. All this time, the Chinese, such as like Yu Gong and his family, have been working together to move mountains. Throughout this long history, with its many changes, legacies such as the story above (known as 愚公移山 *yugong yishan*) were created and philosophies were developed, forming part of China's principles for living.

It is impossible to include here all the philosophies that have shaped Chinese minds; therefore, we distilled a framework to help you decipher the Chinese thought process. The foundation of the framework consists of five core elements:

1. Chinese language—an embodiment of the Chinese philosophy and culture.
2. The law of 阴 *yin* and 阳 *yang*—the law of balancing opposites.
3. Chinese connectedness—the belief that we are "born connected" not "born equal."
4. Midstream living—the golden rule.
5. 面子 *Mianzi* (face)—a concept considered more important than life itself.

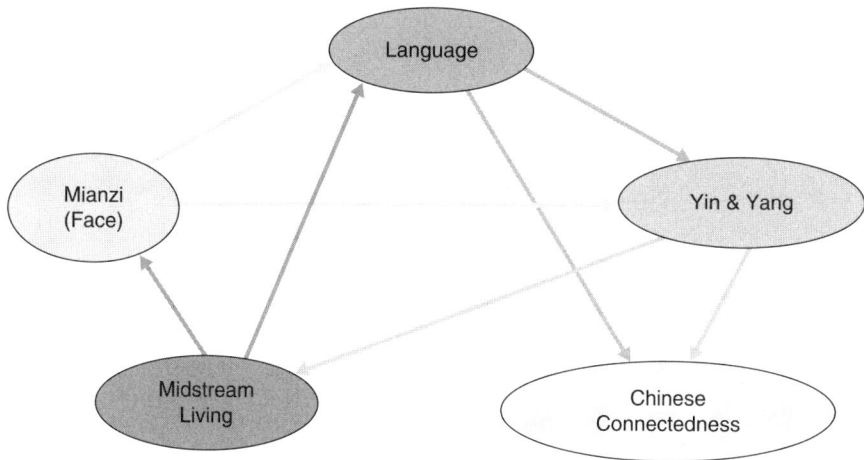

The five core elements

These distinctive elements are very different from those of the West. Not stand-alone concepts, they are interwoven and continuously generate new thoughts and thinking patterns—and will continue to impact generations of Chinese as they form part of the riverbed of the mighty river China.

Lao Zi, the founder of Taoism, said: "A 1,000-mile journey starts with the first step 千里之行, 始于足下 *qianli zhixing, shiyu zuxia.*"

Our first step is to introduce the five elements that form the core of Chinese thinking.

CORE ELEMENT NO. 1: LANGUAGE THAT SHAPES THE MIND

Anyone visiting China will immediately realize that the Chinese have an extraordinary amount of pride in and respect for their own history. Much of that history is kept alive in its languages, and in how the Chinese live their lives and conduct themselves and their businesses.

When Bill Gates first visited China in 1994 to sell his Windows software, he met the then President Jiang Zemin. During that short meeting, Jiang talked about the Chinese civilization and said that Gates should do his best to understand the Chinese language and culture to be able to collaborate more.

Anyone with an interest in China should gain some basic understanding of the Chinese language and the power it has in shaping the Chinese mind. Some view Chinese language as an extension of thought that is deeply grounded in the Chinese culture.

One of the world's oldest written languages, Chinese has barely changed over thousands of years. Today, most ancient philosophies and writings are still widely studied through formal education in their original form with appropriate explanations. More than 40,000 characters are known today. An average Chinese person with a secondary-level education will know how to write and read 1,500 to 3,000 characters. For those with higher education, this number is between 5,000 and 10,000.

How Do the Chinese Learn Chinese?

In contrast to Western alphabets, which are sound based, Chinese characters are symbolic and meaning based. Most characters are pictorial, or at least have a symbolic part that reflects the meaning. Each character is written in a square shape, usually consisting of a symbolic part (the meaning) as well as a sound part (pronunciation). Sometimes, a character doesn't have any meaning unless it is combined with other characters; sometimes, the same character may have multiple meanings.

In addition to the symbolic nature of the language, in the spoken form, Mandarin Chinese has four tones, and Cantonese Chinese has nine! Many characters also sound the same but have different meanings.

In mainland China, every Chinese studies a compulsory subject called 语文 *yuwen*—the character 文 means "culture" and 语 means "language"—from kindergarten to secondary school. During the six primary school years, children learn a few new characters every day while reviewing previously learned ones. In secondary school, learning new characters becomes part of their reading and writing activities.

Reading and writing pictorial characters and learning their various tones means that a Chinese person has a heavier reliance on the right brain. A scientific test has shown that the Chinese use the tone-sensitive right side of the brain to process the tonetic changes in words (in the first 200 milliseconds) before their left brain interprets the associated meaning. Most Western languages, with only one tone for each word, are directly processed by the left brain.

In recent years, much research has been conducted to compare and analyze the different functions of the left and right sides of the brain.

The Chinese EQ

As Chinese written and spoken languages are unique and distinctive, Chinese brains are wired differently from those of people who have grown up with an alphabet-based language that has no tone differentiation.

Often, the Chinese view a situation or business issue in a complete sense—they see the big picture rather than a particular issue. They also see things and come up with solutions based on intuition. We term this the "Chinese EQ" (Emotional Quotient), which has been perfected and practiced for thousands of years.

For example, a famous Chinese scholar once said that the Chinese think with their hearts—hence, in the Chinese character for "thinking," pronounced *si*, 思, the lower half is the character for "heart." The Chinese word for "thinking carefully" translates into "think with your heart" *yongxin sikao* (用心思考).

In Table 2.1, we summarize the three key contrasting aspects between Chinese and Western thinking. A word of caution: It is incorrect to assume that the Chinese are not good at analytical or scientific thinking.

In fact, the Chinese have been learning to apply logical thinking for the past thirty years, particularly in the business environment. It is also worth noting that many of China's highest-ranking leaders came from an engineering background, an education that undoubtedly left a strong imprint on their minds.

Furthermore, in recent years, the Chinese government has been promoting and investing heavily in science-and-technology-focused education. Every year, more than 500,000 university students graduate with engineering degrees, and many more study MBAs both domestically and abroad.

Table 2.1 Chinese and Western thinking

Chinese Thinking	Western Thinking
Conceptual—Uses the "big picture" approach: sees the whole first, then the details; often makes lateral connections from information	Analytical—typically makes decisions based on logic. Uses "one thing at a time" approach: works up to the whole step by step, focuses on details, is often highly organized, makes lists and plans
Listens to HOW something is being said; often prefers "mind pictures" to remember things, doesn't take notes	Listens to WHAT is being said; uses words to remember things, keeps records, particularly figures and numbers
Has trouble prioritizing, often late, impulsive; makes decisions based on feelings; processes ideas simultaneously	Keeps track of time; processes ideas sequentially, step by step; makes logical deductions from information

In the rush to modernize China, both the Chinese government and the corporate sector are learning from Western management systems and theories. Often Chinese executives and entrepreneurs use English acronyms such as key performance indicator (KPI) and human resources (HR). Acclaimed international business and thought leaders, such as Alvin Tofler, John Naisbitt, Bill Gates, Jack Welch, Peter Senge, Edward De Bono, and Phillip Kotler, have large groups of admirers and followers in China.

Most English business bestsellers are swiftly republished in Chinese. For example, the translated version of W. Chan Kim and Renee Mauborgne's *Blue Ocean Strategy* was a bestseller in 2005 in China. Interestingly, in September 2009, the Chinese edition of John Naisbitt's new book *China's Megatrends* was released in mainland China, a few months ahead of the release of the English version in the United States.

The Chinese are also looking at how the Japanese successfully combined their traditional thinking with Western systems of thought to create sustainable communities and organizations.

The Chinese View of Philosophy

Chinese history and philosophy are both embodied and mirrored in the Chinese symbolic language. Generations of Chinese have looked for guidance from philosophers, and mainstream philosophies form the foundation for every aspect of life.

We must highlight that the word "philosophy" has a different meaning to the Chinese. Philosophy provides guidance and principles for their day-to-day living and business conduct. For the Chinese, the exposure to philosophy is broad ranging—from reciting classic essays and reading books in the classroom to the influence of family members and the community. Helen, for example, had most of her induction by observing her grandparents and by reading classical fiction.

The three pillars of Chinese philosophy

In 1948, Professor Fung Yu-Lan 冯友兰 wrote that "the role that philosophy plays in the Chinese civilization is in many ways similar to that played by religion in some other civilizations."[1]

Over its long history, China has nurtured many profound thinkers. Even to name them all would take another book. Here, we focus on three

---

[1] Fung Yu-Lan, *A Short History of Chinese Philosophy*, Edited by Derk Bodde (New York, NY: The Free Press, 1976, p. 1).

of the most important mainstream Chinese philosophies—Confucianism, Taoism, and Buddhism—to provide a general understanding. Each philosophy emerged over 2,000 years ago. In the recent revival and preservation of ancient Chinese culture and teachings promoted by the central government, the three pillars are being restored as the foundation of Chinese thinking.

Confucianism for the country. Confucianism 儒家 *rujia*, the dominant philosophy, emphasizes the importance of social and moral order. Confucius 孔子 (born 551 BC) consolidated the earlier teachings and founded the philosophy. His teachings were later enhanced by various philosophers and were endorsed by most Chinese emperors.

Confucius created a rigid social order comprising five basic relationships and ranked them in order of subordination—ruler and subject, father and son, husband and wife, oldest son and younger brothers, elders and juniors (friends). These relationships led to moral rules and a focus on active participation by man in all matters of the universe. It is crucial to realize that contemporary China is still a hierarchical nation, largely due to the influence of Confucianism.

Taoism. Taoism 道家 *daojia* (or Daoism) stands alongside Confucianism as another mainstream philosophical teaching of China. Tao is the sound translation of *dao*, meaning road or path. Believed to be founded by Lao Zi 老子 (c. 600–500 BC), who lived during the same era as Confucius, it was later further developed by Zhuang Zi 庄子 (c. 369–286 BC).

Taoism, which emphasises the harmonious relationship between a human being and nature, promotes the idea of "non-activity" or "non-action" 无为 *wuwei*, teaching that a person can find contentment in simply being one with nature, and has no need to be actively involved in social affairs, or to interfere with natural matters.

Main differences between Confucianism and Taoism Confucianism encourages people to have a positive attitude, to contribute to society, and to be actively involved in all the roles a person plays. For example, at home, a man should be a good father to his son, a good son to his father, a good husband to his wife; and at work, a good manager to his subordinates, and a good subordinate to his superior. In so doing, a person becomes a sage. Such an attitude is called 入世 *rushi*, a combination of the word "in" and "society." The phrase means "involved" and "worldly."

Taoism promotes a much more passive, "detached" philosophy—one does not have to be too involved in one's social duties, or follow a strict social order. A person can become a sage by finding "the way," through which the highest achievement is the identification with nature. Such an attitude is called 出世 *chushi*, a combination of two characters meaning "out" and "society," that is, "non-worldly."

While Confucianism teaches that a strict social order must be followed, Taoism regards such orders and regulations as unnecessary red tape. Confucianism encourages one to live life in one's righteous place in the family as well as in the society; Taoism encourages one to live away from the crowds and be as close to nature as possible.

Similarities between Confucianism and Taoism Both philosophies recognize the ever-changing nature of the world. The well-known Chinese idiom 物极必反 *wuji bifan* means that once something reaches its extreme, it will turn to the other direction. The best examples are the movement of the moon, and the change between day and night.

The other important similarity between these philosophies is the Chinese "golden rule" 中庸 *zhong yong*, which promotes the art of achieving a fine balance in life, and finding harmony between society and nature.

Therefore, when the Chinese are successful, they turn to Confucianism; when they are less successful, Taoism provides consolation. Care should be taken not to confuse Taoism as a philosophy with the Taoist religion 道教 *daojiao*, which is somewhat different. Similarly, in China, Buddhism as a religion, 佛教 *fojiao*, is different from Buddhist philosophy, 佛学 *foxue*.

Buddhism for the soul. Buddhism has played an enormous role in shaping the mindset of the Chinese people and has had a profound impact on Chinese culture, art, and history. Here, we limit our focus to Chinese Buddhism, mainly as a form of philosophy and a way of life.

First introduced into China during the first century AD, Buddhism gained favor after the collapse of the Han Dynasty (220 AD) and before the Sui and Tang dynasties. Confucianism, Taoism, and other Chinese teachings could no longer provide answers for those living in such turbulent times.

Therefore, many Chinese scholars turned to Buddhism in search of new ways of thinking and inspiration. They were so intrigued by the philosophical and mystical aspects of Buddhism that some became monks to better study and understand the teachings. Rural China embraced Buddhism and localized it as a religion in a more simplified manner. Buddhism reached its height between the sixth and tenth centuries AD during the Sui and Tang Dynasties, a time when many emperors endorsed Buddhism.

The core teachings of Chinese Buddhism promote the development of both compassion and wisdom, and emphasize that one should see the truth in oneself and the world, and be enlightened through self-cultivation and being in the now.

Integration of the three philosophies. Over the centuries, various schools of Buddhism integrated the ideas of Confucianism, Taoism, and other Chinese philosophical teachings. These teachings continued to evolve by inspiring each other for over 1,000 years, until the beginning of the twentieth century. The three teachings form the core of the Chinese civilization. The Chinese term 儒释道 *rushidao* (儒 *ru*, Confucianism; 释 *shi*, Buddhism; 道 *dao*, Taoism) reflects the dominance of their impact on Chinese culture and thinking.

CORE ELEMENT NO. 2: THE LAW OF YIN (阴) AND YANG (阳)—THE UNITY OF OPPOSITES

The core concept of yin and yang originated thousands of years ago. First seen in the 易经 *I-Ching* (*Book of Changes*), the Chinese believe it explains all phenomena related to nature, human society, scientific findings, historical and political changes, scientific findings, as well as natural calamities. Its most popular manifestation is the ever-turning symbol. Yin symbolizes the feminine forces or objects, and yang represents the masculine ones.

There are many schools of thought regarding the far-reaching meaning of yin and yang. Here, we focus on an essential three for the non-Chinese to consider.

1. The universe consists of these two fundamental, harmonious, yet opposite forces. Such forces exist in everything, including the relationship between good and bad, positive and negative. The symbol indicates that things can change and always will. In the business context, today's competitor may become tomorrow's business partner. The secret is to find balance and harmony between people and relationships.
2. The balance between these opposing forces forms the foundation of Chinese thinking. It helps to explain the many seemingly contradictory principles that the Chinese follow. For example, there are sayings that encourage people to help those in need—"to send charcoal to (those in need) in winter" 雪中送碳 *xuezhong songtan*. Then there's the equally popular flip side—"one should only clean the snow in front of one's own house" 个人自扫门前雪 *geren zisao menqian xue*.

    The Chinese are able to live and thrive between the swinging pendulum, balancing a myriad of theories and principles inherited and treasured through generations. A perfect example reflected in the Chinese language is the character 明 *ming*, which means brightness. It combines the character of the sun 日 *ri* and the moon 月 *yue*—balancing opposites.

3. When used individually as characters, yin and yang also have other meanings. To most Chinese, yang indicates something for show or superficial behavior or attitude; while yin indicates the real deal, attitude, or truth that is known only to the selected few.

    For example, a common practice for Chinese-foreign joint ventures is to have two versions of agreements—a yang version designed "to satisfy government or legal requirements" or to gain efficient registration and licenses, and a "yin" one known only to both parties involved that sets out more confidential terms and agreements between the venture partners.

On the following page, you will find the story of Sai Weng, a dialectic. Every Chinese is a born dialectic. You will find a Sai Weng in every Chinese entrepreneur. Not only can the Chinese hold seemingly opposite views at the same time, but also there is yin and yang in each and everything they do.

When things are going well, they are prepared for the tough times ("prepare for a rainy day" 未雨绸缪 *weiyu choumou*); when they encounter difficulties, they tell themselves to be patient because good things are about to come.

When it comes to business transactions, the Chinese will look at the benefits and the negative impacts simultaneously. They will then weigh the two and make a practical decision. They are not worried about negative impacts as they believe that things may change later.

For example, when they see that forming a joint venture with a Western partner will result in more benefits (such as access to technology, financial resources, and management know-how), they will compromise and agree with terms that may be temporarily unfavorable (for example, compromising on management structure or control of their business). Instead of looking at the unfavorable compromise as a setback, they regard the situation as a win-win for both parties.

Yin-Yang symbol

> ### Sai Weng
>
> These concepts are learned early in childhood by studying the famous Chinese fable of Sai Weng 塞翁失马 *saiweng shima*.
>
> Sai Weng lost his horse. His neighbors from the village comforted him and he told them that losing the horse may not be a bad thing.
>
> After a few days, his horse returned. His neighbors said, "You were right in the first place!" Sai Weng replied, "This may not be a good thing."
>
> The next day, his son had a fall while riding this horse and broke his leg. The neighbors said, "Surely this is an awful thing."
>
> But Sai Weng replied yet again, "Not necessarily."
>
> Shortly following the accident, the country called all the young men to fight a war with the neighboring state. Sai Weng's son was not summoned because of his broken leg.

Smart Chinese entrepreneurs also have an uncanny ability to bring out the best in the people who work with them. Always seeking a proper balance in their organization, they hire people who can enhance their skills and fill a void in their own skill sets. Yet they will always make sure that subordinates respect and depend on their leadership and vision; otherwise the smart entrepreneurs will not have a job. It is this constant "natural" tension that defines a skilled businessperson and is one that helps advance the Chinese entrepreneur.

However, there is a negative aspect to such an internally focused exercise. Invariably, when these entrepreneurs work to balance the yin and yang within the organization, they create power struggles and reduce efficiency.

It also makes it almost impossible to nurture an open and trusting culture. Some Chinese employees in these dynamics could spend 70 percent of their energy dealing with internal politics and bureaucratic time wasters. Sometimes, this inward-looking culture forces people to focus increasingly on gaining more power and benefits inside an organization, rather than on expanding or developing the business.

Core Element No. 3: Chinese Connectedness—"Born Equal" versus "Born Connected"

One of our Western friends, Nicolas Morris, a leading economic policy advisor on the Asia-Pacific region, once made a very interesting observation. He said that people in China seemed to be motivated by more than just money, wealth, or individual achievement, and that people in the poorest areas still possessed a genuine sense of contentment and happiness. He commented on an incredible sense of tolerance among the Chinese toward each other.

This contentedness and tolerance stems from the fundamental Chinese idea of being connected. A Chinese person is never encouraged to think in an individualistic manner or attitude, and is never treated on a stand-alone basis. While those in the West may believe that "we are all born equal," the Chinese believe that "we are all born connected."

This belief means that one always lives as part of a network or as a strand in a web. The Chinese society is formed by many networks or webs such as family, work groups, social clubs, associations, and alumni groups. A person has no identity without reference to others to whom they are inextricably linked: A man is the father of his children, a student of his teacher, or a member of the golf club.

This principle has its roots in China's long agricultural history, when the Chinese lived in villages near their fields. For thousands of years, survival depended on people supporting and working with each other, and on the generosity of nature.

Reinforced by Confucian teachings, the concept was extended to loyalty to country (government, for example), and respect for and obedience to teachers and superiors (parents and senior relatives, for example).

The Big I and the Small I

Such conditioning nurtures a strong sense of belonging and patriotism, and a tendency for considerate behavior and sharing, all elements that contribute to contentment. A person who cares only about his or her own achievements is often regarded as being aggressive and selfish rather than ambitious. In Chinese, an individual person is described as a "small I" 小我 *xiaowo*, and in a group as a "big I" 大我 *dawo*.

It is common practice for the Chinese to take up professions or jobs because they were asked to by their parents or assigned by the country (the ultimate "big I"), even when they do not like it. When given orders by an authority (the government, teachers, police officers, anyone in uniform), or by parents or grandparents (when they are the ones who "control" the family), the Chinese always do as they are told.

The Communist Party changed the priorities for most Chinese. Even though family was an important web of the society, it ranked below the country and the people. Many couples lived most of their married lives in different cities because of government assignments, and children were sent to live with grandparents until they reached school age. No one thought of

Mao's Generation

Helen's mother studied Russian during her college days. (At the time, Russia and China were "comrades" and Russian was the only foreign language one could learn—even though few had any chance of using Russian in later life). She was assigned to work in an import and export company a year before graduation; there was a huge shortage of staff during the 1960s when Mao Zedong was trying to find the right economic model for China.

No one ever thought of disobeying such orders or job assignments. In fact, most of them, Helen's mother included, felt honored and proud to "serve the people" 为人民服务 *wei renmin fuwu*, a slogan that Mao created to motivate the nation. Helen's mother happily worked at the same import and export company for more than twenty years, six days a week, with no annual holidays, for a monthly wage of about US$7 (higher than that of many factory workers at the time).

---

challenging or trying to change such decisions, even when they had doubts and questions.

This thinking also prevails in the Chinese business community. The priority for an employee is not to become a star performer, but to find a sense of belonging and become one of the integral links in the web of the company. A manager or employee obeys orders from the superior, and ambitious employees establish "webs" around them that support their career advancement or business ambitions. These webs are not necessarily limited to the workplace—they also function through social clubs or family connections or classmates from school or the army.

For an entrepreneur, such webs—often called 关系网 *guanxi wang*, a network of contacts—provide the most important work and social relationships. When a person becomes very successful or is promoted to an important position, those connected to the person's web will be looked after or promoted as the trusted support group. There is a saying that, "when a new emperor arrives, so does a new government" 一朝天子一朝臣 *yichao tianzi yichao chen*.

Most Chinese business leaders and successful entrepreneurs are masters of building and maintaining a sophisticated network of contacts. They often take advantage of this thinking and manage to find the perfect balance with all parties involved, while also establishing multi-layered boundaries.

> ### *What Microsoft Wants*[2]
>
> In 1998, Microsoft decided to set up an R&D Center of Excellence in Beijing and wanted to recruit some outstanding Chinese graduates. They received thousands of CVs and had to devise a test to identify those graduates capable of "original" thinking.
>
> There were only six questions at the interview:
>
> 1. Why are manhole covers round?
> 2. Please estimate the number of gas stations in Beijing.
> 3. What if you had a different opinion from your teacher?
> 4. If I gave you a difficult question, how would you solve it?
> 5. Please evaluate the user interface of Microsoft's elevator.
> 6. There are two irregular ropes. Each takes one hour to burn. Please burn the two ropes in exactly 45 minutes.
>
> Microsoft believed it was necessary to find free and creative thinkers from the elite of Chinese graduates by devoting questions three and four to seeing how "connected" an applicant was within Chinese society.

However, the negative impact of such connectedness is that individual personalities, independent and innovative thinking, and open communication can be hidden or suffocated.

CORE ELEMENT NO. 4: MIDSTREAM LIVING

The art of achieving balance and harmony in life and with nature is admired and encouraged by the Chinese—and resonates with the idea of connectedness. Termed 中庸 *zhong yong*, we call this "midstream" philosophy the golden rule. It is widely used to balance one's position among a group while maintaining conformity. It is one of the most important "living principles" that all Chinese follow, either consciously or unconsciously. Conformity, while still achieving personal objectives, is regarded as a highest form of contribution to society.

First elaborated in the book *Zhong Yong (The Doctrine of the Mean)*, "midstream" represents what the Chinese call an "ideal way of living." This concept is embraced by both Confucian and Taoist teachings. The author of the *Doctrine of the Mean*, 子思 Zisi, is believed to be the grandson of Confucius, and he wrote the book in approximately 200 BC during the period of the Qin and Han dynasties.

As described in the book, "An ideal person... stands in the center without leaning to either side." *Zhong* means middle, and *yong* means equilibrium.

---

[2] Robert Buderi and Gregory T. Huang, *Guanxi (The Art of Relationships): Microsoft, China and Bill Gates' Plan to Win the Road Ahead* (Simon and Schsuter, 2006).

The Chinese always aim to achieve a fine balance in their work and family, as well as in their social circle. They do their best to stay in an emotionally neutral stage, free of joy, anger, sorrow, or pleasure. Consideration for others is to be remembered and practiced.

This concept applies to many aspects of Chinese life. For example, at home, one maintains a balance between respecting one's parents as well as keeping one's spouse and children happy. In the social sense, one aims to achieve one's personal objectives without using extreme force or means, or to the detriment of others. One should be humble, modest, and know one's place. An ideal person always knows the limits, is in perfect harmony with his or her true self, the society, and nature, and does things in a contented and balanced manner.

The strong sense of conformity in the Chinese community is easily observed and is instilled from a very early age.

In the business context, the golden rule of midstream is unfailingly applied. The Chinese believe that one should behave in a way that is not viewed as too ambitious; on the other hand, one should not be viewed as being lazy or lacking drive.

A school of Chinese fish

A school of Western fish

It is said that when you are too successful in society, in an organization, in your career, or financially, you risk the danger of jealousy, and your superior may be concerned that you are going to overtake him or her; however, you should not be too far behind either, or you won't get anywhere.

Similar to other teachings, midstream also has a negative aspect. Some Chinese misinterpret it in a way that justifies their becoming complacent or passive, often quoting this golden rule. We explain more of such thinking and behavior in later chapters on leadership and work ethics.

It is crucial to understand this concept when one has a large Chinese workforce and wishes to motivate and build a strong cultural bond among employees. This can be used to great advantage in a corporation.

When the Chinese call for a meeting, usually no one wants to sit in the front rows. Sitting in the front is seen as an expression of "I am more important than others." Sitting at the back is disrespectful. Most would find a seat in the middle to keep a safe distance from the front, yet close enough to acknowledge the importance of the meeting and to convey a sense of paying the right amount of attention.

It Starts Early at School

Our young children started kindergarten in the Chinese system at the age of two. The pre-school they attended is run very much like a primary school, and discipline is key. There were more than 30 children in our daughter's class. Whenever Geoff and I dropped her off or picked her up, we found the classroom whisper quiet. Every two-or three-year-old is given clear instructions on how to conduct themselves in a very orderly and regimented manner. The teacher would say, "Don't disturb the others" or "Look how well so and so is doing."

Our daughter now attends the international section of a local Chinese primary school that has an excellent reputation. Upon starting year one, Geoff was keen to understand how she was handling the new school. She claimed to enjoy it, but was a little nervous. Geoff asked, "Who did you talk to at school?" "No one," she replied.

This went on for weeks and Geoff got somewhat worried.
"Surely you speak to someone?"
"No, I can only talk with the teacher's approval. I cannot disturb my classmates and talk to them. And we do not leave the classroom the whole day! We eat and rest at our desks!"

CORE ELEMENT NO. 5: FACE 面子 MIANZI—MORE IMPORTANT THAN LIFE ITSELF

A well-known Chinese nursery rhyme communicates the importance of face:

> 小呀嘛小二郎，背着那书包上学堂，不怕太阳晒，也不怕那风雨狂，只怕先生骂我懒呀，没有学问哎，无颜见爹娘。
> A little boy named Er Lang is going to school.
> He is not afraid of the sun, the wind, or the rain.
> He is only afraid of the teacher criticizing him for being lazy,
> Because if he does not study well, he will lose face in front of his parents.

Helen sang this nursery rhyme as a child. It shows how important learning is in Chinese culture. Interestingly it also reveals the implications of "Chinese face"—pronounced as mianzi in Mandarin. We cannot emphasize enough the importance of mianzi (literally, *mian* means face or surface, although the word itself does not refer to how a person looks).

The concept has been described and analyzed by many Chinese cultural observers since the nineteenth century. Numerous articles and books have been written to explore and explain such a seemingly strange concept. Mianzi is a very difficult concept to translate, even for the Chinese themselves!

Mianzi can be vaguely described as someone's reputation and social status, as well as the image that one establishes in the eyes of others—in some ways, it is similar to a person's "brand"; yet it is also a lot more than that. It forms an integral part of the Chinese way. Intangible, difficult to quantify, yet every aspect of business dealings—from socializing to Chinese banquets to even how the government makes certain decisions—is well informed by this concept.

It is so important to the Chinese that often mianzi is ranked above health or well-being. A good example is a Chinese banquet: To give their guest mianzi, the Chinese will not hesitate to propose one toast after another. In some extreme cases of "face" drinking, the host and guest end up in a hospital having their stomachs pumped!

Due to the sense of connectedness, the Chinese live their lives relative to others. Such interdependency determines that mianzi is a must for everyone. From government officials and successful entrepreneurs to poor farmers, every Chinese treasures his or her mianzi throughout life. For example, a male entrepreneur has many roles to play. At work, he is the owner, the boss in the eyes of his employees; at home, he is a father and a husband; when he socializes, he is a friend. The Chinese believe that life is an opera 人生如戏 *rensheng ruxi*—perhaps because of the constant need to change roles and perform different rituals according to who is watching.

Conditioned by such complex role play and surrounded by multi-layered webs of relationships, the Chinese live their lives subject to the size or the level of importance of their mianzi. Its importance is often associated with work, social status, position in the family, and personal capability. Somewhat similar to the masks (or makeup on the actor's face) used in the Peking opera, mianzi determines how (in this context) important one is, which social circle or class one belongs to, and whether or not one lives a good life. It is the first consideration the Chinese have when they decide what car to drive, where to dine, what school to send their child to, and what friends to choose. Even small things like seating order at a banquet and who gets into the lift first are reflections of mianzi.

Mianzi can have substantial value—multi-billion dollar contracts can be awarded when the decision maker wants to give mianzi to someone; and it can have little value—when someone does not have enough clout, no one will pay attention to his or her requests or orders. Mianzi can grow as one accumulates connections, and advances in life; it can also shrink when one has done something to damage it. One must be seen to be able to "give" mianzi to others where appropriate, and not be seen to be taking away someone else's mianzi. To make someone lose mianzi is considered to be worse than physically hurting them.

As in a Peking opera, a lot of energy is spent around the gesture. Most of such activities are elegant or dazzling to watch—they may not mean anything, yet they can be hugely expensive. At all times, you must be seen (in the context of the Chinese society) doing the right thing and also treating people you are interacting with in an appropriate and considerate manner. It is no wonder then that one of our Chinese friends (the deputy chairman of China's Cultural Promotion Society) calls mianzi "a defect of the Chinese culture."

For example, Chinese families will spend huge amounts of money on banquets for birthdays, weddings, and funerals. The more the guests at the banquet table, the merrier. People who are invited to such important occasions must attend bearing gifts or "red envelopes" 红包, *hongbao*, with money inside. How much one spends on the gifts or how much to put in the envelope depends on the occasion, as well as the relationship with the host. Refusal of such an invitation can be regarded as "not giving mianzi" 不给面子 *bugei mianzi*; the person who invited you will think of themselves as having "no mianzi" 没面子 *mei mianzi*. Therefore, even though all parties involved know what is expected and may hate such exercises, everyone still follows the norm diligently.

From a business point of view, mianzi is vital. Understanding and respecting your Chinese partners' mianzi will have a substantial positive effect on the relationship. However, damaging a person's mianzi (even unknowingly) could mean the end of a friendship or business relationship. We will explain more about how and what you can do to ensure that your Chinese counterpart's mianzi is not "lost" in a later chapter titled "Small Things."

A Glimpse of History

Here is one final word on an important feature of China's background. China's contemporary history is drastically different from that of the Western developed countries. It is important to note that in China, an agriculture-dominated nation, for thousands of years, trading or commercial activities were regarded as inferior compared with farming 重农轻商 *zhongnong qingshang*. Traditionally, government officials were the most important citizens. Successful business people would donate money to obtain a post in the government.

The majority of mainland Chinese were not business-savvy except in some southern regions, for example, in the Fujian and Guangdong areas where the local culture nurtured trading (especially overseas trading) to build personal wealth.

To gain a fundamental understanding of today's Chinese and where they are going, it is necessary to learn where they came from. As we will elaborate in the next chapter, the Chinese have a very different sense and view about time, partly because of their own long history.

Many Chinese believe that China has "7,000 years of culture; 5,000 years of civilization; and 100 years of humiliation." For thousands of years, China was a global superpower, with long periods of social stability, a strong economy, and a great deal of scientific advancement.

However, they also regard the hundred years before 1949 (when Mao Zedong and the Communist Party established the People's Republic of China) as the "period of humiliation." During this period, European powers sought to colonize sections of China as well as Japan, invading and occupying large sections of northern China. Warlords took control of many areas of China, and order and civil obedience fractured and collapsed. It was in this climate that Mao Zedong seized the opportunity to unify China with the introduction of the Communist Party, which has taken China to where it is today.

Given that it is impossible to present a complete account of 5,000 years of Chinese history here, we demonstrate how the Chinese view their own history in the model below.

```
        1949–Now

   100 years of humiliation

    7,000 years of culture
```

How the Chinese view their history

Conclusion

China's unique history and culture have shaped Chinese minds accordingly. It is important to remember that the five core elements identified in this chapter together form the foundation of Chinese thinking, and that each supports and contributes toward the other.

When you are working and doing your best to understand the Chinese, following this framework will provide more clear direction and some useful hints.

Chapter 3
The Emerging Superpower

Crossing the river by feeling for the stones
Deng Xiaoping

Perhaps the best way to comprehend the new China, this emerging superpower, is to imagine a mighty river. It is easy to see the gathering momentum. One truly needs to be here to observe the many businesses and the people running them, and walk through one of the many mile-long Western-style shopping centers packed with thousands of Chinese shoppers. Just a drive from the Beijing airport to your hotel will introduce you to many landmark buildings. Beijing, an extremely large city, is built on a monumental scale. One can be excused for feeling dwarfed by its sheer size—it is designed to have this impact.

When you look below the surface, you will also find that certain things have not changed much, if at all. In this regard, it is vital to remember that China follows its own course, and its riverbed is China's own value system and philosophy.

To borrow from one of Helen's favorite philosophers, Zhuang Zi, the Chinese are "fish" in this mighty river. No matter how turbulent the current may be, the fish intuitively know how to go with the flow. They react effectively, swim fast, and adapt to the many currents and turns.

China's history, culture, and traditions are like rocks in this river, enduring tremendous pressures for thousands of years, eroding slightly, occasionally altering the natural flow. The rocks are solid, reliable, and constant. They give the fish refuge and guidance, and will remain for generations to come.

On first arriving in China, one sees that things are done differently than in the West. China is emerging dramatically onto the world stage and will soon have an impact on all our lives. In this chapter, we do our best to capture what is contemporary China and how the Chinese are coping with their re-emergence as a world superpower.

We outline some essential information on contemporary China to put things into perspective and to help you understand how present circumstances are shaping the Chinese thoughts. We focus on aspects unique to China over the last thirty years, as well as highlight the backdrop of its unbelievable growth and development. In every aspect of the Chinese society, there are conflicting and co-existing 阴 *yin* and 阳 *yang* forces. We propose seven insights to help you navigate the Chinese mind.

Ours is not an exhaustive analysis of China. It is more of a guided tour through the landscape of what a person doing business in contemporary China needs to know. Becoming aware of and appreciating the background of the Chinese you work with will assist you to do well in business without paying a very costly price, sliding into the bottomless money pit, or joining the many whose businesses have failed in China.

100 Years of Humiliation

The mentality of today's Chinese is closely linked to modern Chinese history. Before the establishment of the People's Republic of China by Mao Zedong, China was at a low ebb for over 100 years after colonization began following the first Opium War (1839–1842). The Chinese suffered the combined onslaughts of opium, European economic imperialism, the fall of the last imperial Qing dynasty, a short-lived Republic of China, and a war with Japan—just to name a few difficult periods.

Mao Zedong brought hope to the nation during the first few years of his leadership with the establishment of new China. However, the next twenty years saw the devastating Great Leap Forward and Cultural Revolution. The overarching effects of the Cultural Revolution were extremely damaging. People were encouraged to suspect everything; the education system was brought to a virtual halt, and students and teachers were sent to the countryside to be "re-educated by the peasants." Many intellectuals, including doctors, architects, and lawyers, were sent to rural labor camps. Traditional values and principles were ignored; people were encouraged to criticize cultural institutions and to question their parents and teachers. Countless ancient buildings, artifacts, antiques, books, and paintings were destroyed.

During the Cultural Revolution, much of China's economic activity stalled, with "revolution" being the primary objective. In 1976, China contributed only 1.5 percent of the global industrial production.

Even during the early years of Deng Xiaoping's economic reform, initiated in 1978, the central government became concerned about the changes the reform had brought about, and at times, tried to revert to a controlled economy through the introduction of various policies and regulations. It was not until 1992 that full government support was given to developing a "socialist market economy." During the previous fifteen years, Chinese businesses in all sectors and the society as a whole had been through turbulent times, many suffering greatly from the prevailing political winds of the time.

History in the Making

During the years of Mao Zedong's leadership (from 1949-1976), China was run as a gigantic single economic and political entity with its doors firmly closed to the outside world. All land belonged to the government. Farmers were allotted a certain part of the land to farm, and at the end of each year, they were paid a fixed small amount of money. All businesses in the cities were government-owned, -controlled, and -funded, and were

---

Real People Really Believed

As in the case of the majority of the city dwellers during the 60s to the early 80s, Helen's parents also worked for SOEs. Her father, one of China's first-generation electronic engineers, rose through the ranks to become the Party secretary (the Communist Party leader) of his printer manufacturing factory, Red Star. He remained there for most of his working life, until he was asked by the government to become the Party secretary of a related research institute. In those days (and even today in most SOEs), the highest achievement in one's career was to become a Party leader. Even though most of his time was spent reading Party policy documents or announcements made after national or regional Party meetings, he had no regrets giving up his real work as an engineer. He has now been in retirement for over ten years, living a modest life on his company pension, pursuing his life-long interest in Chinese brush painting.

Helen's mother worked for a textile import and export company in Tianjin for over 25 years, earning about US$7 every month, working six days a week. When Deng Xiaoping announced his economic reform plans in the early 80s, she was appointed a founding committee member of the Tianjin Economic-Technological Development Area (TEDA), one of the earliest development zones that Deng said "has great hope" for the nation. When she first made the move, many thought she was crazy. Even though she made the equivalent of just US$7 a month, it was still more than what factory workers were paid. People who worked for companies like hers were said to be holding a "golden rice bowl"—a very secure job with added benefits such as travel and access to foreign clothing.

known as state-owned enterprises (SOEs). Back then, there was no marketing department, no R&D. An SOE was a social unit. In addition to providing lifelong employment to its employees, it also provided necessary social services to the employees and their families: housing, healthcare, child care, education, and groceries, to name a few.

Under the leadership of Deng Xiaoping, China started its economic growth. Helen still recalls when her mother first took her to visit what looked like a remote, deserted piece of land near the seafront between Tianjin and the port—the future site of TEDA. Her mother looked around at what seemed to be just another poor rural patch in China and said proudly, "one day this will become the most important economic landmark of China."

Today, her dream-like predictions have long become reality. The region's gross domestic product (GDP) surpassed that of the entire city of Tianjin (now ten million people) a few years ago. Even today, there are landfill projects in the region, with billion-dollar investments from both domestic and foreign companies pouring in.

After spending a few years working at her life-long government job, her mother took another brave step. She established her own company in 1983, which classified as a foreign-invested enterprise (FIE). A long-term customer turned investor from Hong Kong helped her to export textiles overseas.

During the early years of the economic reform, before China entered the World Trade Organization (WTO) in 2001, foreign companies were very cautious about investing in China. They were also restricted and limited by Chinese government policy and regulations.

Until the late 1990s, the most common foreign organizations were representative offices and joint ventures (the generation of profit by foreign companies within China was considered illegal, and foreign businesses were required to have a Chinese joint venture partner). Helen's mother was fortunate as she had both local and overseas support that enabled her to operate an FIE, which enjoyed preferential tax treatment.

Now, the regulations have eased and there is a widespread acceptance of foreign-owned companies. Currently, most foreign companies choose to operate as a wholly foreign-owned enterprise (WFOE), retaining all decision-making power and avoiding potential trouble with local Chinese partners. The exceptions are in the banking, telecommunications, and automotive industries, where regulations still govern foreign ownership.

Helen's mother's company was very successful for some years. At that time, few people had the commercial nous to operate privately, as the whole country was run as a giant corporation. Most of her early employees learned the basics from her and soon left to establish their own companies.

Then, in 1992, the word 下海 *xiahai* (dive into the ocean) became very popular after people finally believed that the government would not reverse the course of economic reform. *Xiahai* refers to "diving in" to be a private business owner or to enter a private enterprise.

Like Helen's mother, over 100,000 government officials resigned from their jobs and entered the commercial world. Many Chinese openly expressed their long-suppressed desire for wealth by joining the ever-growing numbers of the early generation of entrepreneurs.

By 2007, more than half of the Chinese companies were privately owned, employing a significant proportion of the entire workforce. They are scattered all over China (more so in the eastern coastal region) and are hugely diverse in terms of products and services. They are the backbone of the new Chinese economy.

WHAT IS HAPPINESS IN CHINA?

During most of the last thirty years, the eastern coastal regions of China have attracted the most foreign investment and enjoyed the most dramatic economic growth.

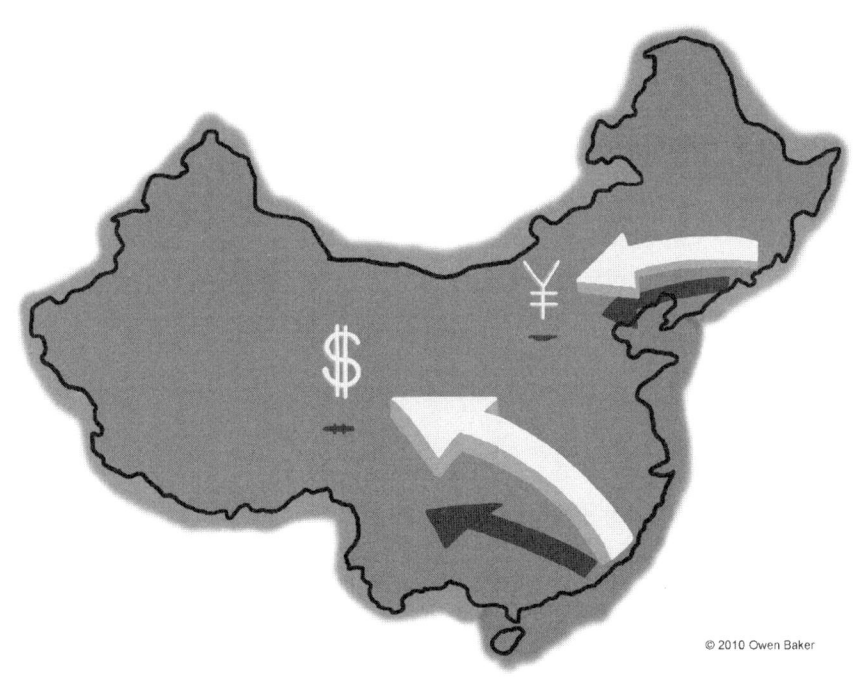

Going West

These regions cover only a small proportion of the vast Chinese landscape. Western regions started to catch up with the coast after President Jiang Zemin declared the great initiative of "developing the West" in 1999. The central government has invested over US$13 billion in the region every year to improve infrastructure, including more than 10,000 km of new expressways and thirty airports. Cities like Chongqing in Sichuan Province, with its thirty million people, and Wuhan in Hubei Province are emerging as the fastest growing hubs for business and urbanization.

Part of the reason China was not affected as adversely by the global financial crisis in 2008 as many had expected was the continued investment into these western regions from both central and local governments, as well as from private and international business communities.

Even though happiness may mean different things to different Chinese, nobody questions the economic growth and the improvement of living standards in the last thirty years. The country's gross purchasing power (GPP) has grown more than tenfold. Measured on a purchasing power parity (PPP) basis, China in 2010 stood as the second-largest economy in the world behind the United States (although in per capita terms, the country is still a lower middle-income one, and according to the United Nations, over 200 million Chinese still fall below the international poverty line).

It appears that the vibrant and constant energy of building an economic powerhouse has supercharged the entire nation and its people. In fact, it is said that when one is away from China for six months, one is out-of-date. Changes happen constantly in every aspect of life, business, and the surrounding environment. Laws and regulations are introduced daily; businesses come and go; and even restaurants that one frequents can disappear or transform into another business overnight. Helen still remembers how on

Is It All Relative?

Our Chinese friend Sanli recently went back to her hometown in Northern China, one of the many beneficiary cities of this recent development. She came from a small city in Inner Mongolia, a few hours by train from Beijing. When she caught up with a relative who had recently moved into her city from the nearby countryside, Sanli asked if she was happy with her new urban life. "Of course," she said, "There is a tap in my kitchen and a tub in the bathroom—I have 24-hour access to water inside my apartment!" Helen recalls her own excitement in the early 90s when she first moved into a Beijing apartment that had two taps—one with hot water twenty-four hours a day!

one occasion, the direction of a major one-way street was reversed overnight, causing considerable confusion!

One positive impact is the many leapfrog opportunities that exist in the Chinese economy. A typical example is the rollout of the Internet and wireless technology. In a very short time, China built an advanced telecommunications structure with comprehensive coverage nationwide. By the end of 2010, out of the 457 million Internet users, more than 300 million used mobile devices to access the Internet.[1]

Today, there is approximately 8,000 kilometers of high-speed railway across the world. From having no high-speed trains only a decade ago, China now has a few thousand kilometers of high-speed railway successfully linking major cities. The ten-hour train journey between Wuhan and Guangzhou has been cut to just three hours via a new bullet train travelling at 350 kmph. By 2014, China will have 13,000 kilometers of high-speed rail that links forty-two cities, surpassing the cumulative length in the rest of the world.

CHINA INSIGHTS

The following seven China insights serve as a set of tools to gain a better understanding of the contemporary Chinese and what is inside their minds.

China Insight No. 1: The Chinese Definition of Freedom and Democracy

Unlike some Western countries, every single major development in contemporary China has been brought about first by political power—via the central and regional governments. The Chinese have a very different view and understanding about freedom and democracy. While much has been discussed about human rights and the freedom of the Chinese people, it must be noted that these terms mean different things to different people—even more so when it comes to a country like China with its unique culture and historical traditions.

The Chinese believe that we are all born connected, that every individual is part of a whole. Harmony and balance are what the Chinese strive for, rather than the Western sense of total individual "freedom" which to the Chinese means constant disharmony. Furthermore, for a Chinese person, the status of one's 面子 *mianzi*, face, is far more important than being right.

While the Chinese admire many things about the West, it has to be said that the Western political system isn't one of them. They see that Western

---

[1] http://www.chinanews.com/it/2011/01-19/2796311.shtml; http://www.chinanews.com/it/2011/01-19/2796297.shtml, (last accessed, April 2011).

governments attempt to resolve issues using war and aggression rather than diplomacy, which in the eyes of the Chinese is the most uncivilized way of conflict resolution. The Chinese believe that a win-win solution should always be the ultimate goal in such situations, rather than focusing on who is right and who is wrong.

John and Doris Naisbitt, in their book *China's Megatrends* (2009), propose that in China there exists a different type of democracy in which "… the leadership frames a broad concept for the society as a whole that incorporates bottom-up ideas, initiatives, and demands. Top-down and bottom-up initiatives are then established and encouraged to adjust flexibly as conditions and circumstances require, all in the context of the overarching common goal set by the leadership. This creates a vertical structure, with a constant flow of ideas and experiences up and down the hierarchy. China is … creating … a democratic model that fits Chinese history and thinking … its major strength is that it releases politicians from election-driven thinking and permits long-term strategic planning."[2]

It is apparent to many who have been to China that the Chinese are actually happy with their lives and the opportunities available to them. The Chinese government has done its best to provide a mix of business freedom and centrally controlled security measures, even though some may seem unacceptable to Western commentators. It must be remembered

---

Is Freedom Relative?

At a business lunch, Geoff was seated next to a smart, well-educated Beijing business-woman who owns a profitable private business. Geoff asked if she was happy with her life. "Of course," she answered, saying that she could buy anything she liked, had the freedom to travel wherever she liked, and do business with anyone. When Geoff asked if she felt free, she again said, "Of course." She could do a lot more than her parents could in the past, and her wealth was beyond her parents' wildest dreams.

Geoff asked how she could be really free if she could not go out on the streets and demonstrate or protest.

She looked at Geoff quizzically and said, "Why on earth would anyone ever want to do that!"

---

[2] John Naisbitt and Doris Naisbitt, *China's Megatrends*, 1st ed., (HarperCollins Publishers, 2010).

How Time is Controlled

One thing the Chinese central government does control is the way time is spent. In recent years, the government decided to allow its citizens to have more leisure time. For years, there was a six-day work week, with Sunday as the public holiday. In an effort to help the nation adjust to the rate of change and also to encourage travel (in order to boost the hospitality and travel industry), the government changed the work week to five days, and scheduled three "Golden Week" holidays. In 2008, the government further modified this by reducing the Golden Weeks to two and shortening the third week to three days—to encourage people to spread their holidays throughout the year.

The two major holiday periods in China are Chinese New Year (generally around the end of January or early February) and National Day (October 1). There are also five three-day holidays throughout the year: the Chinese New Year holiday, Tomb-Sweeping Day, May Labor Day, the Dragon Boat Festival, and the Mid-Autumn Festival. As these national days and festivals often fall on weekdays, the weekend before the holiday period is turned into working days, and people are expected to work both Saturday and Sunday to have the benefit of a five to seven day break after the allocated holiday period. People are expected to work for their holidays! The Chinese take it all in their stride and abide by government's directions.

that there are 1.4 billion people in China. To satisfy all their needs is, to say the least, a challenge.

China Insight No. 2: How the Chinese Mind Has Been Stretched

As so much has happened in China within such a short period of time, many conflicting phenomena coexist. For example, people were quick to obtain credit cards in urban China following the development of the banking industry in the last five to ten years. China was previously a cash-only society. Helen still remembers that when she went with her mother to buy a car in 1985, they had to carry a suitcase full of cash!

Today in China when you make a credit card transaction, you will receive an SMS notification on your mobile within seconds. However, due to the still relatively inefficient banking system (which is going through dramatic changes as we write), you need to queue for up to an hour when you go to a bank branch to pay your monthly credit card bill!

We examine below some of the internal and external "stretch factors" and their impact on Chinese thinking and attitudes.

Internal stretch factors

Taking advantage while the good times last. In light of the constant changes the Chinese have experienced and endured, they want to make the most of the situation before any potential shift in policies. Despite political consistency since 1992 that brought increasing confidence to the business community, past social and economic turbulences contribute to the urgency of getting things done as quickly as possible—while the good times last!

Successful entrepreneurs and astute Chinese are all excellent "wind surfers," able to read the direction of the wind intuitively and adapt swiftly. For example, in 2008, as part of the stimulus to combat the global financial crisis, the Chinese government waived the profit tax on properties that people had owned for over two years. In early 2009, there was a rumor that the preferential tax treatment would end soon. All across the country, people started buying their properties, particularly in major cities such as Beijing, Shenzhen, and Shanghai, causing a sharp increase in housing prices.

On December 9, 2009, the Chinese government did announce its intention to end the preferential treatment by the end of the year, extending the period of ownership from two to five years. The trading volume of property skyrocketed. The local government offices dealing with property ownership transactions had to work during the weekend to handle the huge volume of transactions—a rush that came to a halt at the beginning of 2010. The "surfers" of the property policy "wind" are now resting happily with their wins of yet another change.

The will of the people. It is universally known that the Chinese are hardworking and willing to embrace change. An almost explosive

Case Study: *Global TechCo's Long March—Winds of Change*

Carl, the young Chinese opportunist, was riding his own winds of change as he wooed Global TechCo and its founder. He knew that both the Chinese central government and local governments were investing aggressively to attract new technologies, particularly in the area of green energy.

As China strives to embrace alternative energy, billions of dollars are being poured into new industry and new technology. Global TechCo was an ideal partner for a Sino-foreign joint venture. The new business could attract millions of dollars of grants from the various levels of Chinese governments.

entrepreneurial energy can be felt everywhere in China. People flock from the countryside to the coastal cities or from cities to overseas to find work and earn money. After years of hard work, some return to their home villages or cities to continue their accumulation of wealth, investing in regional areas.

For example, in 1990, there were approximately 250 million people in the eastern coastal regions. By 2008, that number had grown to more than 400 million. In Beijing alone, the population is nearly 20 million, of which 5 million are non-residents working in a booming economy.

Urbanization has been fueled by the migration of people from the farming areas to cities in search of higher income, a better living, and better education for their children. In 1978, fewer than two million migrant farmers worked in the cities. According to the Ministry of Agriculture, that number has grown more than fifty times to over 100 million today.

A Personal Story

Zhan Qingzhi, our *ayi* (nanny), is a typical example of the many migrant Chinese workers in the eastern cities. She came to Beijing from a remote area of Anhui Province about ten years ago when the wave of "going into the city" started in her hometown. As was the case for many from the rural areas, she could not complete her secondary school education due to the family's financial constraints. She first arrived in Beijing clueless about what she was going to do and tried various temporary blue-collar jobs before settling into a full-time nanny role.

She and her husband are among the fortunate few who can both work and live in Beijing. Her husband is a carpenter and works on various jobs, sometimes as a contractor for a construction company, sometimes on his own to renovate people's apartments. They live together with her elder sister, who also works as a nanny, and her husband. Recently, our nanny helped her sister to find a job in our neighborhood.

Every day, they ride their bikes together for over fifty minutes from the village where they found cheap accommodation, as they save every possible dollar for their children's education, as well as for their families back in their hometown. These villages in Beijing are slowly being taken over by property developers to build high rises as Beijing continues its rapid growth and expansion. The house she was renting earlier was about thirty minutes away from work. One day, she was told abruptly by her landlord to move as he needed the land for redevelopment.

When we first hired Zhan Qingzhi, her mother and father ran a convenience store near her residence in Beijing, and helped to look after her ten-year-old daughter who went to a local school for a few

(*Continued*)

(*Continued*)

years after paying a "donation" of about US$1,200. This was required as she was not born in Beijing. The Chinese have identity cards called *hu kou* issued in the town or city where they are born. The system restricts people from the rural areas from enjoying benefits provided to the urban population, including insurance, housing, and education. Until recently, it was difficult to move about within China and find jobs in other cities under the *hukou* system.

Her husband's parents and siblings still live in their hometown. She and her family have returned to their hometown only once in the past four years—for her father-in-law's seventieth birthday. Her younger sister moved to Shenzhen, a city in Guangdong Province of southern China, with her child and husband.

Early in 2008, our nanny sent her daughter back to the hometown with her parents as the the *hukou* identity system would not allow her to sit for the higher education entrance exam in Beijing. If she goes back too late, she may not be able to catch up with the local standard, which is much more competitive than that of large cities like Beijing.

Desire to "go out." This term in Chinese is referred to as 走出去 *zou chuqu* or "go global." In recent years, the Chinese government has been encouraging businesses and people to go abroad.

The rapidly growing number of overseas destinations has been attracting millions of Chinese tourists. More than 45 million Chinese joined overseas tours in 2009, a twenty-fold growth from 1992. According to the World Tourism Organization, that number will reach 100 million in fifteen years.

The other fast-growing group going overseas is Chinese students. From 2001 to 2008, over one million young Chinese became overseas students. As most Chinese parents will do anything to provide the best education for their children, fueled by the resulting improved earning capacity, the trend will no doubt continue in the foreseeable future.

In the business arena, China has been making a significant effort to expand globally. The country's annual outward investment grew from virtually zero in 1979, when China embarked upon its open door policy, to US$913 million in 1991, then to US$4 billion in 1992, the year Deng Xiaoping made an important tour to southern China to reaffirm China's commitment to its reform and open door policy.[3] The trend has been

---

[3] Leonard K. Cheng and Zihui Ma (2007), "China's Outward FDI: Past and Future," http://www.nber.org/books_in_progress/china07/cwt07/cheng.pdf, (last accessed, October 2011).

continued ever since. According to the Ministry of Commerce, in the first quarter of 2011, China made direct investments totalling US$8.5 billion in 974 overseas enterprises of 98 countries and regions around the world.[4]

Some of the outgoing investment efforts are through mergers and acquisitions. One high-profile example is the computer manufacturer Lenovo that acquired IBM's PC division in late 2004. Another equally high profile example is the state-owned energy conglomerate China National Offshore Oil Corporation's (CNOOC) failed attempt to acquire the US oil company Unocal.

The failure did not stop the increased trade winds that sent more Chinese overseas. The government is determined to see more national brands join the global elite. Companies nationwide observe, learn, and reflect upon others who have had overseas experience. It has also made more Chinese aware of how cultural differences and effective communication play vital roles in dealings overseas.

External stretch factors

International investment—the foreign wolves. A huge and constant inflow of foreign investment has been fueling growth in China and is likely to continue. China continues to be ranked by most international firms as their preferred investment destination.

The Chinese have mixed views when it comes to foreign investment and foreigners doing business in China. Before the 1990s, only a very small percentage of Chinese had the opportunity to work with foreigners or foreign companies. As a consequence, the attitude toward foreign investment was greatly influenced by the media, comments and policies of the Chinese government, and by personal experiences from people within business or family circles. However, for the majority, foreign investment—and more importantly, its impact on and further implications for their personal lives—presents a steep learning curve.

Many believe that allowing foreign investment into China is the right thing to do. It has enabled China to achieve phenomenal economic growth and has brought some of the best technologies and practices from around the world, lifted the country out of poverty, and broadened the horizons of many Chinese. In general, foreign companies operating in China offer higher salaries and better career prospects than the Chinese counterparts.

On the other hand, some have concerns. When China was admitted into the WTO, there was an anxious debate on whether local businesses would survive "when the foreign wolves arrive." Many fear that foreign businesses would drive local businesses into obscurity.

---

[4] China's outbound investment tops 8.5 billion USD in first quarter. http://english.peopledaily.com.cn/90001/90778/90861/7356287.html.

Another Chinese concern is the "invasion" of Western values and beliefs. Some argue that the contemporary Chinese society has already gone too far in adopting "all things foreign" instead of preserving its own cultural heritage.

A third concern is that, as the purpose of a foreign company is to maximize financial returns, it may pay scant regard to the welfare of the Chinese community. Foreign investment could also lead to accelerated pollution, and the demise of Chinese competitors.

Demand from different time zones. Chinese businesses have to operate twenty-four hours a day, seven days a week, to trade with the rest of the world. Many Chinese companies regularly correspond with their overseas partners who have eight to fifteen hour time differences with China. At the moment, China is still very much an export-driven country. Manufacturing accounts for over 60 percent of China's economic growth. In fact, a US economic consultancy has forecast that China will overtake the United States as the world's largest manufacturer in 2020. As the "world's factory," it is difficult to have time off. Even though China is making huge efforts to turn itself into the "world's laboratory," the change is unlikely to happen overnight.

Case Study: *Global TechCo Long March—A Foreign Wolf?*

While in the past, Global TechCo would have been regarded as a foreign wolf, it is now clear is that the foreign technology company is coming to China for some obvious reasons:

1. Considerable money is available from the Chinese government to support green energy initiatives;
2. Sufficient private funds also support the development of technology; and
3. The speed to market and the enthusiasm such companies can harness in China, together with the willingness of the Chinese to break through old bureaucratic systems so business can get done, attracts more foreigners to China.

Also, Carl, our Chinese opportunist, is willing to dance with the foreign wolf because he believes he holds the financial strings. Global TechCo's world-leading technology is unavailable in China. If Carl can persuade his friends and government contacts to invest, and if Global TechCo is willing to establish operations in China, then he can play on his own turf to better control the outcome.

One of the most "connected" nations. In 2010, China had over 457 million Internet users, over 66 percent of whom (303 million) accessed the Internet via their mobile phones. Some young Chinese have two mobiles—one for calls and the other for playing games.

China is arguably the best in the world in terms of its effective use of mobile phones by banks, businesses, and government departments. For example, during her recent trip to visit a client in the Tianjin Binhai New Region, Helen received an SMS from the local government welcoming her to the area and offering support in her business endeavors.

Technology has been a catalyst for China's globalization. Even though some are yet to fully adopt email as a communication tool, many do leave their mobile phones on all the time, and will respond to phone calls and text messages speedily.

China Insight No. 3: Remain Fluid in China Time

Living in Beijing during this fast and furious time can be oppressive and draining. Sometimes we feel that we are sitting on a giant wheel of fortune—the non-stop spinning can be unsettling and exhausting.

Business is running in high gear to catch up with the West. Meetings can be held at midnight, during the weekend, or on holidays. There appears to be no reason to put them off to another day.

What distinguishes the China buzz from that of a city like New York or London is that it is not restricted to the central business district of a capital city. The buzz resonates across the whole nation in hundreds of cities, some of the largest in the world.

The Chinese cope with this by staying fluid and being flexible. It is very important to bear this idea in mind when one is planning a business trip to China. When scheduling meetings, a week or two in advance will be good enough to lock people in. Planning earlier than this is simply not possible, since people's schedules change on a daily basis as they cope with "China time." We must say, it was difficult at the beginning to get used to such a different sense of time and planning, but we are now very comfortable with meeting calls or invitations from friends and business associates with a day or two's notice.

China Insight No. 4: Apply the PRC Alternative

The law of *yin* and *yang* means that the opposite can also be true with regard to China time. Due to China's unique and long history, people believe that time will settle many problems. A common belief is that given enough time, any issue or conundrum will run its course toward resolution.

The dangers inherent in moving too fast are best captured by the Confucian saying, "The quicker you want to go, the further away you will be from your destination" 欲速则不达 *yusu ze buda*. Many Chinese adopt a careful and conservative approach when it comes to dealing with new things or testing out a new way of conducting business.

The Chinese sense of time stems from China's agrarian roots. The Chinese calendar moves to the rhythm of nature and follows the agricultural timetable rather than the Roman calendar. The lunar month follows the movements of the moon. The annual festivals originate from harvesting, resting, and planting. The Chinese New Year, for example, is the Spring Festival—it celebrates the time to start planting crops.

There is genuine appreciation for this natural rhythm, even though it may seem a little slow to the West. While China may be a rapidly developing world economic power, it will not lose its agrarian roots entirely. For those who wonder how anyone could ever accomplish anything in China, remember that the PRC (People's Republic of China) can also stand for **P**atience, **R**elationships, and **C**ash.

Mountains of Documents, Oceans of Meetings

Such a long history also brings bureaucracy. China's vast land and population was managed for the emperors by an equally vast number of bureaucrats. The Chinese have made bureaucracy an art form. Even today, the government strives to reduce the "mountains of documents, and the oceans of meetings" 文山会海 *wenshan huihai*.

The number of steps for a simple banking transaction, let alone a business start-up, can leave a person pen-weary from filling out forms and completely befuddled by the process. One wrong step can create week-long delays. Even at parking lots, one sees the attendants filling in forms, recording the license plate details of cars coming and going!

The modern army of bureaucrats is trained regularly on how to devise and follow processes and procedures. The time wasted navigating these processes leaves one questioning how anything gets done in China. The Westerner sees bureaucrats as persons who deal with the public dismissively while moving at an excruciatingly slow pace.

For example, setting up a wholly foreign-owned company in China can take three to six months, if you are lucky! In the West, the same can be done in the space of days—and in some jurisdictions, hours. Even though the government has been streamlining various departments and amalgamating duplicated units across the nation's political and administrative system, the bureaucracy left behind by the "controlled" economy era remains.

China Insight No. 5: Contacts and Connections Matter

By now, you may be wondering how such massive changes can occur, and how can they take place so quickly. Even though bureaucratic delays happen on all fronts, there is another army that thrives at beating the process and bending the rules. Approvals are spewed out the back end as fast as they are put in the front.

While to a Westerner, the time it takes to process and submit forms may qualify as glacial speed, the Chinese treat it as a mere formality. This is also where *mianzi* (face) and 关系 *guanxi* (connections) play their part. As long as the decision makers at various levels have given the green light, paperwork and formalities can be almost irrelevant. Furthermore, in business settings, deals are often struck before the formal structure of a company is established.

When you are working with Chinese partners, they will usually be able to achieve the impossible without making a fuss. Also, there are professional "paper shufflers" (agents) who make a living by getting the forms right. They go to various departments to get all the necessary permits and licenses—and believe us, the cost is worth it.

China Insight No. 6: Have you 山寨 *Shanzhai*'d Today

Recently China coined a new word—*shanzhai* (pronounced "shan-jai"). Its literal meaning is "mountain village," but it has acquired a new meaning since 2008—any type or form of imitation. In today's China, there is a whole shanzhai world. There are shanzhai products and online games, a shanzhai culture, and a shanzhai economy, to name a few. It is so popular that some people say to each other, "Have you shanzhai'd today!"

The word shanzhai was first used to describe no-brand mobile phones and their manufacturers, which came into existence in 2003. Most major Chinese mobile phone manufacturers failed to supply quality, innovation, better products, and adequate, inexpensive after-sale services. So shanzhai phones became very popular. They cost a fraction of the price of their competitors, are multifunctional, and look just as trendy.

Helen recently met a young American IT professional, who had just acquired a shanzhai mobile. He was so proud of it that he could not stop talking about all the functions while showing off the phone. I could hardly see the back cover as he had put many fake logos on it—including those of iPhone, Nokia, and LG!

Even though this term originated in mobile phones, the shanzhai phenomenon has somehow caught the imagination of millions of Chinese netizens, who have made shanzhai an interesting layer of the Chinese contemporary culture. Without the Internet, there would be no shanzhai.

For example, one manifestation of this phenomenon is shanzhai events. Among the best-known ones are the online Shanzhai National Spring Gala (which parodies the most popular Chinese New Year show—CCTV's *New Year Gala*—broadcast live on the eve of each Chinese New Year), and the Shanzhai Nobel Prize event. Note that both imitate high-end, popular yet authoritative events—"grass-roots party for the grass roots," as one of the organizers put it.

There are also shanzhai celebrities. Many shanzhai singers perform in underdeveloped places, where people can neither afford nor do they have access to the performance of actual celebrity stars. These events are very successful, even though the audience knows that they are not getting the "real" thing.

This phenomenon is causing much heated debate both inside and outside China. Many (both Chinese and Westerners) have expressed their concerns, saying shanzhai products and events are shameless acts of piracy or purely profit-oriented operations. The supporters, however, have openly praised the "shanzhai spirit"—the ability to imitate and improve, to speed delivery to market, to make products and events affordable to many, to innovate where possible, as well as add a sense of fun and spoof wherever appropriate.

Like it or not, shanzhai has become part of life in China. We will further explore this unique subculture in the chapter on localization and intellectual property.

China Insight No 7: Diverse Chinese Minds

China is not a monocultural country. More than 1.4 billion people from fifty-six ethnic groups speak eighty dialects and live in many different cities and regions. A good comparison would be to think of China as America—and treat it accordingly as a collection of diverse subcultures within a common boundary. Just as people from the East coast do not behave exactly as those from the West coast, similar regional differences exist in China. For example, people in Beijing are different in many ways from those in Shanghai. China is one of the most diversely populated countries in the world.

Ethnically, the Han people form the largest group, numbering 1.1 billion, 93.3 percent of the country's population. The other fifty-five ethnic groups are called ethnic minorities, including Muslims and the Jewish who settled in China a very long time ago, and whose descendants now speak Mandarin and regard themselves as Chinese.

Over 67 percent of the Chinese are aged between fifteen and sixty-four years. It has been said that due to the one child policy and other social policies, China is growing old before it is becoming rich. Also, the majority of the population resides in the eastern coastal region. According to official data, as compared to 170 million in 1978, China's urban population increased to 575 million by 2009. There are more than 117 cities in China with a population greater than one million people.

The generations of Chinese

While in the West there are the baby boomers, followed by Generations X and Y, in China, they are categorized as the post-50s, -60s, and -70s (that is, those born in the 1950s, 1960s, and 1970s), and so on. For ease of reference, we describe the generations as pre- and post-Cultural Revolution generations, and then the younger generations, born in the latter part of the 20th century.

Pre-Cultural Revolution. Those born before the mid-1950s were deeply affected by events surrounding the Cultural Revolution. The educational system was brought to a halt, and almost all teachers were sent to rural labor camps. The government sent many people from urban areas to live in the countryside as farmers.

This era also had serious implications for the ranks of middle management. Many professionals and managers were sent for re-education and relocated to farm areas, leaving a considerable gap in the workforce as the economy grew, following China's re-emergence. This is why many of today's partners, senior managers, and business leaders are only in their forties.

Post-Cultural Revolution. Those born in the mid-1950s to mid-1960s, while being slightly affected by the political upheavals of the time, had little recollection of the starvation and social decay of the period. These people have become the new leaders and are significant drivers of change and regeneration powering the emergence of China.

Post-1960s and post-1970s. Those born in the late 1960s to 1970s, while still touched by the late years of the Mao Zedong era, were the first to experience the freedom resulting from the opening up of China. These people, the new young leaders, are slightly more radical than those from the Post-Cultural Revolution generation, and are significant drivers of change.

Little emperors and empresses. The younger generation, born in the late 1970s to 1980s, is the result of the single child policy introduced in the late 1970s to restrict parents from having more than one child. The policy has been significantly relaxed as of late. This generation, part of today's workforce, is generally regarded as being self-absorbed. They lack a sense of responsibility, have little awareness of traditional values, are spoiled as a result of receiving undivided parental attention, and are overly burdened with two parents and four grandparents to support, a duty traditionally shared among siblings.

Bird's nest generation. The term was given to the Chinese born in the 90s, as over one million of them volunteered for the successful 2008 Beijing Olympic Games. Not only did they show the world how friendly the Chinese are, but they also somewhat surprised their fellow Chinese by showing a sense of responsibility and collective honor, pride in the traditional culture, faith and confidence in the economy, and were a great credit to the government.[5]

Differences between the post-70s, -80s, and -90s. People from the post-70s and post-80s are seen as being relatively materialistic. Those from the post-90s express individuality and self-expression in a non-conforming way. For example, many from the post-90s adopted an online language called "Martian Language," whose words are a combination of English letters, Chinese characters, Internet slang, and symbols. Since most teachers and parents are unable to understand this new language, it has become an effective way for students to keep their communication private. It also gives them a sense of identity.[6]

Sea turtles and seaweed. During the Cultural Revolution, no mainland Chinese was allowed to travel or study overseas. A select few travelled to Russia and were soon called back due to the souring of relationship between the two countries. The Chinese who were living overseas were not allowed to enter China either. The doors to China were closed to all foreigners. Only during the past thirty years has China let its "best and brightest" study and work abroad, allowing them to catch up with Western developments. Many who left China for education have now returned to their homeland.

The initial returnees (mostly aged between 35 and 50) were welcomed with open arms, regarded as sea turtles—returning home to help China rapidly progress. These sea turtles were much sought after, obtained good jobs, and were highly prized.

However, as the number of returnees grew, China realized that not everything in the West was worth adopting. Therefore, those who had prospered from this growing wave became less admired and less sought after by employers. The description changed from the admired sea turtles to the not so popular seaweed.

---

[5] http://www.slideshare.net/chinayouthology/kungfu-issue-2bird-nest-gen-presentation.
[6] "Martian Language" heats up among Chinese teenagers," http://news.xinhuanet.com/english/2008-05/22/content_8225456.htm, (last accessed, April 2011).

ABCs. Many Chinese live outside China. Those who are first or second generation migrant Chinese in Australia and America are often called "ABCs" (Australian or American Born Chinese). Some may have been brought up with a Chinese cultural background but may not speak or understand Mandarin. Most grew up with minimum or no exposure to mainland China, so care needs to be taken by non-Chinese when working with them in mainland China. Often ABCs may have as many cultural and business barriers to overcome as a non-Chinese visitor!

Hong Kong, Macao, and Taiwanese Chinese

It is important to note that the mainland Chinese do not regard Hong Kong, Macao, or Taiwanese Chinese as fellow citizens. This reflects recent historical upheavals. For forty to fifty years, mainland China, Taiwan, Hong Kong, and Macao were separated, with barely any communication or cultural exchange. Hong Kong was regarded as a British colony that would eventually be reunited; Macao, a small, colonized island, would also eventually be reunited; and Taiwan to this day, remains a political hot spot that receives much political attention and generates consternation.

Before the Hong Kong handover in 1997, the mainland Chinese people were not allowed to visit Hong Kong. An increasing number of mainland Chinese now visit Hong Kong and Macao as tourists; however, cultural integration remains in its infancy. Only since 2009 have there been regular direct flights between Taiwan and the mainland. It is still very difficult for the mainland Chinese to obtain visas to visit Taiwan. Even though there are many active and successful Hong Kong and Taiwanese business people in China (an estimated 500,000 over Taiwanese work and live in Shanghai alone), it is important to remember that, to the Chinese, they are still regarded as foreigners. Considerable care needs to be taken when one conducts business in the mainland; bringing a Chinese colleague who has a Hong Kong or Taiwanese background may create more misunderstanding, especially in the northern part of China.

CONCLUSION

So how are the Chinese themselves coping with all this change and upheaval? The catchphrase "crossing the river by feeling for the stones" by Deng Xiaoping is famous among the Chinese. We see it as a perfect motto for contemporary China.

Remember that this is the first time in a long period that the Chinese are facing uncharted waters. The skills they cultivate are dramatically different from ones that Westerners rely on, and Chinese businesses are at the very early stage of mastering globalization skills.

There have been many failures and many successes as companies regroup and remain flexible. Chinese companies surge along, reinventing themselves, learning in every possible way, at times, with little regard for the casualties. Many are keenly in search of answers, mostly through trial and error—the only way they know.

A Grain of Salt

As you begin to contemplate the new China, keep in mind this story (or urban myth) we that heard some years ago:

A CEO of a large multinational company was at a dinner banquet with the then Shanghai mayor. When asked about the effect of communism on the growth of China, the mayor stood up and grabbed the salt shaker, slowly removed its top, and with a sweep poured the salt in the shape of a dragon across the large wooden dining table.

He exclaimed that all the grains of salt represent 5,000 years of Chinese history. He then carefully picked up one grain and flicked it across the room, saying, "That grain is fifty years of communism!"

Chapter 4

Chinese Leadership

The beam that sticks out rots first
Anonymous

In the Spring and Autumn period (770–476 BC), the famous strategist Sun Wu (better known as Sun Zi) came to see the Emperor of the State of Wu, bringing along his great military treatise, The Art of War. *He offered to help turn the State of Wu into a more powerful state by strengthening its army through better training.*

The Emperor was not quite convinced and asked, "Can you try your method out on my small, ill-disciplined army?"

"Yes," said Sun Zi.

"Can you try it out on some of my women?"

"Why not?" said Sun Zi.

The Emperor called 180 concubines and ordered Sun Zi to train them and make them into a strong army. Sun Zi organized the young ladies into two teams and appointed two of the Emperor's favorite concubines as team leaders. Everyone was given a weapon and they stood in line.

Sun Zi asked these women, "Do you know how to march forward, backward, to the left, and to the right?"

"Yes, we do!" they replied.

However, Sun Zi thought it would be best to explain in great detail how to march in each direction. He also told them time and again that they must obey orders and explained why it was so important.

Sun Zi beat the drum and ordered his little concubine army to march to the right. To his disappointment, the young ladies, who had never received military training before, did not act as he had ordered but instead giggled and skipped around. Sun Zi did not blame them and said in all seriousness: "It's the general's fault when he hasn't made himself clear." So he repeated several times what he had said moments before.

He then beat the drum and gave an order to march to the left. Again, the ladies giggled instead of taking his order. This time, Sun Wu said seriously: "The order was clear. It's not the leaders' fault that no one obeyed!" He immediately ordered that the two concubine leaders be beheaded!

The Emperor, who was watching, was shocked and immediately sent someone to plead mercy for his favorite concubines. But Sun Zi rejected the pleading. On his insistence, the two team leaders were executed. Sun Zi then appointed two new concubine team leaders and proceeded with the training.

This time, all marched perfectly, obeying Sun Zi's orders, just like skilled drill soldiers.

From then on, the troops of the State of Wu were trained by Sun Zi and became the strongest in the region.

The Chinese and Westerners view leadership differently. In this chapter, we examine how some Chinese view leadership and compare it to the Western view.

We define leadership in the Chinese context and explain how all the five core elements have their impact on the Chinese perception of leadership.

Admittedly, many Chinese managers are not leaders in the true Western sense—they either have the power given to them or micromanage their business to the extent that nothing can be decided when they are absent. However, China would not be where it is today without a great number of political, business, and intellectual leaders. We will introduce some of the most influential Chinese business leaders and share their extraordinary stories and insights.

There are many potential leaders in China. We leave you with suggestions on how to identify, nurture, and develop them within your organization, or how to work with them as business partners.

DIFFERENT PATHS, DIFFERENT LEADERS

Each of these broad business groups mentioned below creates different types of leaders by offering drastically different career paths. In a state-owned enterprise (SOE), leaders are those who master the skill of aligning their political interests, commercial interests, and personal objectives harmoniously. The leaders of private businesses primarily focus on commercial viability as well as the growth of their businesses; being politically correct is still an issue but secondary. Leaders in the foreign-invested enterprise (FIE) context are motivated to advance their careers in ways similar to those of Western business people.

In contemporary China, Chinese businesses are broadly categorized into three groups:

1. State-owned enterprises (SOEs)—including SOE subsidiaries and related businesses
2. Private-invested enterprises (PIEs)—private Chinese companies

3. Foreign-invested enterprises (FIEs)—foreign-invested companies, including wholly owned enterprises, joint ventures, and representative offices.

The SOE Sector

Some managers have risen to very important executive positions after spending most of their working life in the same organization. Typically, they share many characteristics of the previous generation. Because of their longevity within these organizations, they are usually extensively connected and command a high level of loyalty from their subordinates.

Other managers have been hired from outside these same SOEs, frequently handpicked by the government or the previous leader. Often, these managers are highly educated and have both MBA degrees and extensive experience dealing with the international business community. Some are overseas returnees. As compared with the internally promoted executives, they are more flexible and open to learning and working with Western partners. However, they know that it is the government that has given them their position and power, both of which can easily be taken away.

The PIE Sector

The rapidly growing economy over the past 30 years has sent waves of opportunity to many talented entrepreneurs. The emergence of the early generation of private business owners is closely linked with Deng Xiaopeng's economic reform. They cluster around the coastal cities—the first participants of the "get rich first" movement. During the very early stages of reform, most entrepreneurs operated restaurants, convenience stores, or other small-scale businesses so small that those who made it were called 万元户 *wan yuan hu,* a person who had more than RMB 10,000, approximately US$1,250.

In the early 2000s, a second generation of entrepreneurs flourished. Most of them had stronger commercial, financial, or operational knowledge than the earlier group. They came from various backgrounds, and were able to build their businesses into substantial organizations. Their prior SOE experience (if any) had little impact on their management style, and most of them were talented, strong business leaders who established some previously non-existent industries. They were young, energetic, and remained commercially focused while carefully maintaining political support. They shared many of the leadership elements we described previously.

It is worth noting that some built significant businesses without much international competition in a market that needs almost every kind of quality service or product. Other entrepreneurs in the PIE sector leveraged the low cost advantage and government incentives to engage in lucrative export businesses.

Encouragingly, there is also a small group of entrepreneurs who have built successful companies, some in the technology and financial services sector. Most of them have had substantial exposure to the international environment, speak English fluently, are highly qualified, and have no trouble working with Western business executives.

The FIE Sector

Most mainland Chinese managers in the FIE sector are called "professional managers" (职业经理人 *zhiye jingliren*). Some are overseas returnees who have spent considerable time working with international businesses. Others have made a career change from a typical SOE environment for various reasons (special care needs to be taken when dealing with this particular group, as the transition into the Western culture may not be easy).

Different Generations of Chinese Leaders

Chinese decision makers can also be divided into the three groups defined by their generation: pre-Cultural Revolution, post-Cultural Revolution, and young leaders.

We look at each of these groups in detail below.

Pre-Cultural Revolution

Most decision-makers of this generation have an engineering or manufacturing background, or have no higher education and come from rural China. They have been through the Cultural Revolution and have spent a long time in an SOE environment.

This generation usually holds very important positions in SOEs or large PIEs. More often than not, they are long-term Communist party members or they hold positions in the government. Their uncanny ability to be politically savvy, balance various relationships, and take calculated commercial risks makes them hugely successful. A couple of legendary leaders in this category include Liu Chuanzhi, who founded Legend Holdings (later renamed Lenovo), and Fu Chengyu, CEO of the China National Offshore Oil Corporation (CNOOC).

> ### Godfathers of Chinese Entrepreneurs
>
> Mr. Liu Chuanzhi was born in 1944 and has an engineering degree from Xi'An Military Communications Engineering Institute. He was a researcher in the Computing Technology Institute of the Chinese Academy of Sciences before he and three colleagues founded a small company in 1984 to sell printers and computers. Today, that small company is the largest PC manufacturer in China.
>
> While actively running the investment arm of the Lenovo group, Mr. Liu is also the vice-chairman of the All-China Federation of Industry and Commerce, and deputy to the 10th National People's Congress. Widely respected as the "godfather" of Chinese private enterprises, he remains active in both Chinese and international business arenas.
>
> Mr. Fu Chengyu, born in 1951, has become one of the most westernized Chinese business leaders. He has a master's degree in petroleum engineering from the University of Southern California and is amongst the few from his generation with overseas education. He was also given permission by the government to work as the vice president in an American company's Chinese joint venture (Phillips China). Mr. Fu worked in many of China's oilfields before moving up the management ranks.
>
> He joined the China National Offshore Oil Corporation (CNOOC) in 1982 and was appointed president in 2003. In 2007, he also became a member of the Central Commission for Discipline Inspection during the 17th Communist Party of China (CPC) National Congress. Fluent in English, Mr. Fu is one of the most high-profile yet modest business executives running one of the largest SOEs in China. When Helen visited CNOOC, she spoke with the young Chinese guard about his boss. The guard expressed how hardworking, personable, and friendly Mr. Fu is. He arrives at work earlier than 7:00 a.m. and always stops and talks to him with a genuine sense of interest and care.

Post-Cultural Revolution

Between the pre- and post-Cultural Revolution generations, there are no well-trained managers due to the tragic impact of the Cultural Revolution. Nonetheless, the post-cultural revolution generation makes up the majority of today's Chinese business decision makers. More leaders will emerge from this group in the next ten years.

Younger Generations

There are not many senior decision makers in this age group yet. The exceptions are those who have inherited businesses from their parents, or those who have tapped into the technology or IT industries. Often, they are offered managerial positions upon their return from the parent-funded overseas education, or they become involved in creating new, popular technology.

China's Donald Trump (Listen Only to Yourself!)

One star entrepreneur is Jack Ma, founder and CEO of Alibaba, one of the world's biggest B2B online marketplaces. From the time when he first set up Alibaba over ten years ago, almost every step he took was viewed by others as "crazy," "impossible." Today the online portal boasts over 61 million users and had a revenue exceeding $870 million in 2010.[1] Ma believes the secret is that he only listened to himself.

Born in 1964, Ma has a degree in English from Hangzhou Normal College in Zhejiang Province. He was the first Chinese entrepreneur to appear on the cover of *Forbes* magazine.

In May 2009, Jack Ma was named by *Time* magazine as one of the world's 100 most influential people. CCTV awarded Ma Entrepreneur of the Year: Business Leaders of the Decade, a highly influential award in China. His company sponsors the reality TV show "Winning in China" (similar to Donald Trump's Apprentice), one of China's most watched TV series. He personally appears on the program as a judge.

In an interview with *Time*, Ma says he handled early difficulties by being flexible. "There were three reasons we survived," he once said. "We had no money, no technology, and no plan." Coming from such a state of "nothingness," Jack Ma has our respect for his almost magical leadership.

Build Your Own Dream (If Others Can Do It, So Can I!)

Wang Chuanfu was born into a poor rural family of seven siblings in 1966. His parents passed away when he was in high school, and his eldest brother supported his education. It took him fourteen years to build his company BYD into one of the most promising electronic vehicle manufacturers, and to become the wealthiest Chinese in 2009. World spotlight shone on him, particularly after Warren Buffet invested in his company.

After obtaining a master's degree from the Beijing Non-Ferrous Research Institute in 1990, he worked as a government researcher for a few years before establishing his own company that made better batteries for electronic products. Instead of using fully automated equipment, he trained all the workers. In quality control, he broke every job down into basic tasks and applied strict testing protocols. By 2002, BYD had become one of the top four manufacturers worldwide—and the largest Chinese battery manufacturer.

---

[1] "Alibaba's 2010 Annual Report," http://img.alibaba.com/ir/download/201104/2010_Annual Report_ENG.pdf, (last accessed, October 2011).

He then acquired an automobile manufacturer in 2003, moving into what appeared to be a saturated market. Using an approach similar to the one that brought him his previous success, he reverse-engineered the car manufacturing process to rely on manual operation. Today, his company hires more than 100,000 workers and more than 10,000 engineers. In 2009, a BYD sedan called the F3 became the bestselling car in China. Helen's brother received one as a wedding present from his parents-in-law. The newlyweds really liked it because it is gas efficient, spacious, and easy to park.

Described as "a combination of Thomas Edison and Jack Welch" by Warren Buffett's friend and long-time partner in Berkshire Hathaway, Charlie Munger, Wang does admit that he is not very democratic when it comes to making corporate decisions. Reputedly, he once said, "Who knows more than I do (inside the company)? 98 percent of my decisions are correct."[2]

Ma Huateng, China's Bill Gates

In China, on the lower-right corner of almost every computer screen, one can see a little "penguin," which is the Tencent QQ—an instant messaging service button. The head of this giant "penguin kingdom" is Ma Huateng, a seemingly shy and introverted young man born in 1971.

CEO Ma, who founded Tencent in 1998, graduated from Shenzhen University in 1993 with a degree in computer science. In ten years, his Tencent QQ (the Chinese instant Internet-based communication tool) became the largest instant communication service network in China, with an estimated 93 million users in 2009. He ranked first in the IT category on the Hurun Rich List 2009 (a listing of the 1,000 richest Chinese). The valuation of his company (in the world of Internet businesses) comes third after Google and Amazon.

At the 2009 CCTV Business Leaders of the Decade Award program, he said, "It took us a year to have 10,000 users when we first started. When we had 10 million users, I thought perhaps we had reached the limit. Now I can see that we are going to create a miracle—together with all the Internet users out there: 100 million Tencent customers."

Interestingly, he was not sure what to do before establishing Tencent. "I felt it would be something related to the Internet. I know I can succeed in anything I put my mind to."

When asked about the secrets of the stellar success of Tencent, he gave a very Chinese answer—"It's about seizing a whole host of random opportunities—we were just very good at 'taking punches' on this journey of exploration."

---

[2] "Warren Buffett takes charge," http://money.cnn.com/2009/04/13/technology/gunther_electric.fortune/, (last accessed, May 2011).

WOMEN WHO SHAPE CHINA

Mao Zedong once said, "women can hold up half of the sky" 妇女能顶半边天 *funu nengding banbiantian*. He ended the unequal treatment that women had received for thousands of years in China. However, it was not until after the economic reforms that China started to see a generation of powerful women. According to a Chinese government white paper, the urban workforce is now 42 percent female.

Today, female entrepreneurs form a major part of China's economy. Rupert Hoogewerf, who compiles the Hurun Rich List in competition with the Chinese Forbes' ranking, said that most of China's female entrepreneurs are of first generation and that their stories embody the history of modern China.

On the 2009 list (with a cut-off valuation of $150 million), there were 102 women, representing 10.2 percent of the total. More interestingly, Chinese women now account for more than half of the world's richest self-made women.

In China One Can Realize Any Dream

Sitting in her large, sunny, ultramodern office east of Beijing, Zhang Lan, founder of the South Beauty Group, summarized our meeting with a strong opening. Huge pictures of her decorated the walls. One was taken with the Himalayan Mountains as the backdrop; she was facing away from the camera, wearing a tasteful and colorful outfit. Her long hair was swept high in the air, and her posture spoke quietly of confidence in where she was heading.

Zhang Lan grew up in Beijing without her father, a Tsinghua University professor. By the time she was born in 1958, he had been discredited as a rightist and was forced to live in a shed.

A decade later, during the Cultural Revolution, her mother, a state official, was labeled "an intellectual." That meant a one-way ticket to the countryside for "re-education." Zhang spent her youth in rural Hubei Province before returning to Beijing Business College, then went to work in a cousin's restaurant in Canada. In 1991, armed with $20,000 in savings, she came back to Beijing with her young son and opened her first restaurant.

Now she is the chairperson of the well-known chain of South Beauty restaurants. She has been voted one of the "Ten Most Influential People in China's Food Industry," as well as one of the "Top Ten Most Influential CEOs in China."

On leadership, her comment was, "When a chef does not listen, I tell him to move over and I do it myself. So I set a strong example right from the start."

Creating an Enterprise after Retirement

Although she has not appeared on the lists of the rich in either *Forbes* magazine or *Hurun*, Guan Yuxiang may be the richest self-made Chinese woman who started a business when she was 60 years old.

Guan retired as a saleswoman for a state-owned gas and electric meter company at the age of 55. At 70, she is now the chairperson of China's largest privately owned can manufacturer, with annual sales of US$210 million and an annual growth rate of 30 percent.

Guan believes that getting older simply means a new stage for opportunity and strength, and she proved it by getting an MBA at the age of 65.

In 1991, she went to the small province of Hainan, China's second largest tropical island in the south, which had been designated as a "special economic province" in 1988. Thanks to local government support, Guan set up her can manufacturing company with a low-interest loan of less than $300,000. She used the loan to buy the land and build the plant, and then used her own savings to purchase equipment.

So what does this petite only daughter of a rural family say about leadership and her success? In her opinion, it is essential to learn how to be an upright woman before doing business.

"A good conscience is a soft pillow."

China's Oprah Winfrey

Widely considered to be China's wealthiest self-made woman, Yang Lan has been described by *Forbes* magazine as "one of China's 50 most successful entrepreneurs." The Paley's Center of Media (Museum of Television and Radio) honored her with a "She-Made-It" award in 2007 to recognize her achievement as a TV journalist. Yang's mother was born in Beijing and worked as an engineer while her father taught English literature and occasionally acted as the official translator for former Premier Zhou Enlai.

In 1990, Yang was chosen from over one thousand women to be the co-host of a new variety show on TV, "Zheng Da." It was China's highest-rated program with 220 million regular viewers. Despite being one of China's most well-known TV hostesses, Yang left China in 1994 to pursue a master's degree at New York's Columbia University.

After completing her degree, she returned home to join the Phoenix Chinese Channel. While her two popular programs generated more revenue than any others on Phoenix, in 1999, she left and co-founded Sun Television Cybernetworks with her husband, Bruno Wu. The company eventually became Sun Media Investment Holdings Limited, with business interest in television production, newspapers, magazines, and online publishing.

(*Continued*)

> (*Continued*)
>
> How did she successfully break through so many corporate and cultural barriers? "I like creativity," she said in an interview. "I would rather fail at creating new programs than succeed by making ones from old and tired ideas."[3]

LEADERS AND DECISION MAKERS— THE CHINESE DEFINITION

So how do the Chinese view leaders and leadership? The two illustrations below provides a visual depiction of how it differs from the Western concept.

Western leadership

Chinese leadership

---

[3] http://www.shemadeit.org/meet/biography.aspx?m=161.

> **Case Study: *Lessons from Global TechCo's Long March***
>
> China has not had sufficient time to develop in-depth corporate experience, so most Chinese do not understand how a company board operates, let alone a company with a multiplicity of shareholders appointing professional management.
>
> In our Global TechCo's Long March story, unbeknown to the Chinese team (and more importantly, unbeknown to Carl the middleman), the founder had long been reduced to a very small shareholder in the company as several venture capitalists had invested in and controlled the company. He had little influence on their decisions.
>
> A few years ago, the Global TechCo Board hired Tom, after an extensive worldwide search for an internationally experienced CEO. Tom was assigned the responsibility of guiding the company forward in the commercialization of the technology. In effect, Tom had to make all operational decisions.
>
> Such a situation is rare in China. Usually, it is the founder who controls and makes all the important decisions in a Chinese company, regardless of his/her management experience or current title.
>
> Whether the founder had taken advantage of this misconception, or whether he had not openly communicated with the Chinese that he wasn't the "real boss," his behavior led to fatal consequences, as we shall see.

Indeed, the Chinese understanding of leaders is very different from the commonly accepted definitions in the West. For example, the word "leader" in Chinese simply means "someone who is in charge" (领导 *lingdao*).

Also, the Chinese often confuse or address people with authority or power as "leaders," as traditionally, the decision makers in society, government, and various areas in China are called "leaders." The other word for leader is 领袖 *lingxiu*, literally meaning "collar" and "sleeve."

LEADERSHIP—THE CHINESE DEFINITION

Leadership has a completely different connotation in the Chinese mind as compared with the commonly accepted Western concept; that is, the ability to guide, direct, or influence people. Dr. Xisu Wang, a Chinese friend who wrote a book in Chinese on leadership, reflected upon the fact that leadership is a fairly new concept in China. The word did not exist in Chinese until about a hundred years ago, and it was the Japanese who brought the concept to China. Once again, it is important to understand that one hundred years may mean a long time in countries such as the

United States, Canada, and Australia. In China, however, this is merely "a bend in the long river of Chinese history" 历史长河的一瞬 *lishi changhe de yishun*.

Traditionally, leadership is linked to political power. Historically, it is important to remember that, for most of China's 5,000-year history, its society was led by emperors—self-made rulers, typically, who started a new dynasty. As soon as a new dynasty was established, the ruler did everything in his power to ensure his family was in control for as long as possible. Naturally, any sign of real and non-royal leadership was viewed as a threat. The prevailing government used both military and social forces to keep such competition at bay.

As a result, in the eyes of most Chinese who grew up in the era before China opened its doors to the world, whoever has authority or power automatically becomes the leader, regardless of his/her ability to influence people. In essence, this means that many people who have little or no Western leadership qualities can become leaders. This authority can be obtained through political power, money, connections, corruption, and force, to name just a few means.

In more concrete terms, generally, the Chinese from the post-60s to post-80s adopted this mentality because for generations, leaders had been imposed upon them. The leadership skills of such people are hardly questioned—their position is respected, not their skills. However, younger Chinese are showing signs of different thinking and are beginning to challenge such patterns and hierarchy. More often than not, they are demanding true leadership in their superiors and the world around them.

THE SOE SYNDROME

Recently, a major international mining organization expressed its frustration to us with regard to their China operation. They are faced with challenges and problems with their senior Chinese managers who exhibit many of the following weaknesses:

- They are not proactive.
- They don't identify their own solutions, and are always asking for direction from above; they lack leadership qualities.
- They don't plan ahead.
- They don't take responsibility or accept accountability for their actions (always blaming someone else).
- They don't follow or develop systems; instead, they manage issues on an ad hoc basis.
- They ignore problems and do not act until it is too late.

The above are problems faced by many foreign companies in China. We call this the "SOE syndrome" as it stems primarily from the SOE background and training. Other contributing factors include the Chinese history (both ancient and contemporary), and China's educational and cultural frameworks.

Clashing Leadership Styles

While the above issues have been lurking in the China operations of many international companies, leadership has also become a vital issue for more and more Chinese companies that are going global, acquiring overseas firms, and running their overseas operations the Chinese way.

Working for a Chinese Boss

Gary was the only foreigner employed in a completely Chinese private enterprise. They hired him because their main clients were multi-national companies, and the young Chinese business owners realized that the business had grown beyond their depth of experience. They wanted to become a global company and establish branch offices outside China.

Gary was employed to head a major new department to help integrate Western culture, leadership style, and management principles. The expectation was that eventually, his department would spin off to become the listed vehicle of the group. However, in less than a year, he decided to leave, as he was frustrated by the fact that his leadership had been constantly undermined by other Chinese managers and the owners.

He explained this perfectly in his resignation email:

> "I have reconsidered my decision to leave. After our many discussions on leadership and management, and the many reports I shared with you over the past year or so, it is obvious to me that I cannot create and deliver a professional business service in the Group. My leadership is undermined, and the direction is continually changed even after discussion and general agreement. I try to put plans into action, only to see them changed, reversed, or ignored. I have lost all confidence, in just the same way as the team has lost confidence in me.
>
> I thought you were looking for a leader to work with you. However, I find that I am working as a junior manager, waiting for directions to change, seeing instructions going to my team members to perform duties that are in conflict with my own directions, and when I advise my team of decisions (particularly these past few months), they ignore me and wait for the next change from the leadership (above me)."

Conversely, not only do foreign executives suffer from such different perspectives when managing their Chinese managers, but also the same problems exist when private Chinese enterprises employ expatriate executives to help manage their Chinese operations.

What is the reason for this? The Chinese employees in this company were following who they believed was the "real leader." They waited to hear from the person with "authority" rather than their supposed "leader" in the business unit. Insufficient authority was given to the foreigner (who was a highly skilled Western manager/leader). The Chinese owners always interfered in the running of the business unit by issuing instructions that cut across the organizational structure that they had previously set up.

SOEs AND THE ULTIMATE LEADER

We cannot emphasize enough that true Chinese leadership (authority) resides only in the hands of the government. Most successful business leaders and entrepreneurs reached their positions because they were either favored by the government as managers of large SOEs, or because of their ability to ride the momentum created by the government in pursuit of the nation's economic growth.

The Government Decides When It is Time for the Chairman to Go

In late June 2007, Chen Tonghai, chairman of Sinopec (Asia's largest oil refinery group listed at the Hong Kong Stock Exchange, ranked No. 9 in the *Fortune 500*, 2009) suddenly "resigned" for personal reasons. The announcement was made by both the State-owned Assets Supervision and Administration Commission of the State Council (SASAC) as well as the Group Company.

There were rumors that he is now under "double supervision" (*shuanggui* 双规, a newly created term which originally meant that a corrupted government official or business executive is confined under government supervision, and given a limited amount of time to confess). Clearly, the government made the decision for him for reasons that outsiders will never know.

SASAC announced that the person replacing him was Su Shuling, deputy general manager of PetroChina, Sinopec's main competitor. The prevailing rationale was that the central government was not happy with the management of Sinopec, and was hence sending a strong message by replacing him with someone from the competitor.

> ### *The Government Can Change an Entire Management Team in the National Interest*
>
> Only two companies in China are licensed to operate the landline telecommunication networks nationwide—China Telecom and China Unicom. In late 2005, the central government announced that the senior management teams of the two companies would swap. The former CEO of China Telecom was instructed to run competitor China Unicom's business! The government explained that it wanted to make sure that there remained a fair degree of competition and cooperation between the two organizations!

Despite the effort that the Chinese government has put into inviting foreign involvement in the economy, there remain a few industries that will always remain tightly controlled or monitored. Resources and telecommunications industries are among them.

Leaders of the SOEs know that they are not self-made leaders. They mind and manage the state assets (in the form of an ever-expanding business) on behalf of the government. Even though a small percentage of them may own shares in the company because of the recent move toward initial public offering (a government decision to enable some major SOEs to take advantage of the stock market boom), their first priority is to see that the government is pleased with the operation. As we shall discuss later, many CEOs of large SOEs are also senior members of the Communist Party, and hold positions in the central government. All commercial decisions are made after carefully considering political, social, and personal implications. If they lose their political career, they will lose everything.

CHINESE LEADERSHIP STYLES

No. 1: Top-down Management

Most Chinese business leaders adopt a top-down management style, even more so in the case of the PIEs. Some say Chinese entrepreneurs treat their businesses as their wives (that is, nobody else but they themselves can look after the business). Usually, orders are given and decisions are made by the CEO or chairman, regardless of the size of the business, a situation quite similar to what our lone expatriate friend, Gary, experienced in the large private Chinese organization.

The TCL Story (Part 1)

Mr. Li Dongsheng (chairman and largest shareholder of TCL Electronics—a major listed Chinese electronics group regarded as the first Chinese company to go global), lately openly admitted that one of the key mistakes he made in TCL's European operation was to ask a Chinese friend of his, who had almost no international corporate business experience, to head the operation. (TCL has since filed for bankruptcy of its European operations after suffering huge losses since the acquisition.)

Important decisions are usually made with no explanation or the least amount of communication possible to get buy-in from the middle managers or business unit leaders. Of course, staff members are not consulted. Employees are simply expected to follow the decisions made by those in command. No questions are asked; no feedback is sought.

When it comes to operational issues, a manual for employees is rare. Even if there are rules, they are not always implemented. Protocols are mostly established in an intangible way, and new staff learn such un-written rules by following those who have been there longer, or by following a confidant of the owner if they are able to build such a connection.

Power always resides with business owners. There is a clear understanding that it is their business and their money. They may consult with their confidants or their network; however, they will make their own decisions.

No. 2: Make No Mistake about Who's the Boss

The senior management group usually serves as "supporters, advisors, or counsel" to the business owner, while middle managers are people temporarily "parked" there to be either promoted or demoted. As a consequence, any decisions or changes made by them will most likely be ignored.

Remember that in an organization, the Chinese will apply the golden rule, 中庸 *zhong yong*, and balance their position among the group while maintaining conformity. This means the employees will follow the leader's beliefs and management practices to promote harmony and swim midstream.

It is All in the Title

Jeff, a good Chinese friend ours, worked for a large private energy group near Beijing. Ten years ago, the founder of the business failed to get into the university after three attempts.

He then formed a small gas tank delivery company with three staff members. Now, the group has annual revenues of US$200 million supplying natural gas to a number of major cities.

Most of the senior management were people who joined the company when they (including the founder himself) were all riding tricycles delivering gas tanks. The only exception was our friend Jeff, an ex-management consultant hired as the international "figurehead." He has a very fancy business title of "Managing Director, International Business." Yet everyone knows that he doesn't have any real power. Real power resides in the hands of the founder, and no decision will be made without his sign-off.

No. 3: Micromanagement Common

It is a common belief among business owners that too much information can confuse and divert expected outcomes. Each employee is expected to do his/her job, ask no questions, and show no initiative.

Small- and medium-sized Chinese organizations are generally micromanaged to such an extent that middle management barely survives. Leaders get involved at every level of operation and want to make decisions at all stages. Eventually, the constant cutting across all layers of management functions can create disarray and employee apathy or inaction.

No. 4: Communication Based on the "Need to Know"

Over time, most Chinese employees perfect the art of mind reading, that is, guessing what the boss is thinking and working within undefined frameworks. It is very unusual for a Chinese leader to make frequent speeches

The Boss Handles Everything

A few years ago Helen worked with the CEO of a large SOE subsidiary with over 400 staff members, assisting the company to form international strategic alliances securing multi-billion-dollar contracts.

During one of the trips she made with the CEO back to China from France, he got on the phone while the plane was landing to arrange the pick-up cars and organize the logistics for the French guests who were travelling with them! Besides being the "logistics manager," the CEO also signed all paychecks for all senior and mid-managers. When he was travelling (as he often did), everyone simply had to wait for his return.

to the entire company. Getting buy-in from your own staff might be seen as a sign of weakness or losing "face" in front of your subordinates—rather than as better communication and stronger leadership skills.

This again stems from the Chinese historical and cultural traditions. There are sayings such as "when you speak too much, you are highly likely to make mistakes" 言多语失 *yanduo yushi* and "true meaning cannot be defined by words, it can only be perceived by intuition" 只可意会, 不可言传 *zhike yihui buke yanchuan*.

Often, business owners also give very brief, sometimes even encrypted, instructions to identify close allies in the subordinate group. Those who interpret exactly what is expected from them and perform well have a very good chance to be promoted.

Leaders can also feel exposed or at a risk of being less admired by their employees when they say too much or get too close to their employees. They are much more comfortable communicating on a need-to-know basis with their most-trusted employees. Most will create an image of a loner above the employees.

Many Chinese leaders have come to rely on their business acumen and informal and non-systemic information gathering to make decisions rather than the formal data-gathering and analysis used in the West. They take pride in their successful decisions and keep their decision-making process and keys to success private.

The TCL Story (Part 2)

Li Dongsheng says that he has had strange experiences in the United States and Europe where TCL has acquired companies. He feels uncomfortable when his foreign managers whip out charts and talk about the problems their units face in ways that seem dry and intangible—and then volunteer solutions as if there was no need to consult their senior managers.

Globalization for the company is exciting. "But of course, there's a lot of pressure and we have to learn a lot of things from scratch," Li says. "When we have meetings with executives from China, they say something is good or bad and I know what's going on. But foreign managers, they say, 'We're facing a loss of $10 million and here's the answer,' and I can't tell if they are right."[4]

---

[4] Based on a Chinese article by Fu Guolai, titled "Nine reasons why TCL suffered huge losses", *IT Times* (Chinese), 5 January 2007.

THE IMPACT OF CONFUCIANISM

We mentioned Confucianism earlier as one of the core elements. The Confucian concept of moral wisdom was a predominant force in China, endorsed by most emperors throughout Chinese history, from the first-century BC until the mid-20th century, just before the Cultural Revolution (1968–1978). The over-arching influence of Confucianism extends into political, social, educational, and cultural arenas. Confucius' teachings underlie how the Chinese see an ideal human being, how such an individual should live his life and interact with others, and the forms of society and government in which he should participate.

Perhaps to some people in the West, Confucius is the subject of an innocent joke or the start of a good saying. However, it must be remembered that, in China, Confucius is much revered and even though most Chinese will not react to such light-hearted references, they will interpret such behavior as lack of respect for the Chinese culture and China in general.

During the Cultural Revolution, Confucianism was criticized as a "feudalist, superstitious thought." However, there is a recent revival of interest in the teachings of Confucius, and many Chinese business leaders and entrepreneurs diligently follow the principles. Most of today's Chinese manage their businesses using the "emperor/minister" or "father/son" model based on Confucian teaching.

The current government has also endorsed this trend and as a result, the Confucian teachings are now widely studied in most Chinese universities. Also, since mid-2006, CCTV (the broadcasting group owned by the central government), has broadcast a series of lectures on Confucius and his teachings. Special mention should be made of Professor Yu Dan of Beijing Normal University who conducted a seven-part daily series of her own personal interpretation of Confucianism on the program "Lecture Room."

The program was so popular that Professor Yu became an overnight celebrity. In December 2006, she published her first book in Chinese based on that popular lecture series (The English version, *Confucius from the Heart: Ancient Wisdom for Today's World*, was published by Atria in 2009). On the first day of the book launch in Beijing, she autographed over 8,000 copies, and more than 12,000 copies were sold on site from a single bookstore. Sales reached 800,000 copies within the first month, and have now reached five million, and are still growing. The book is one of China's all-time bestsellers.

To elaborate on Confucianism and its impact would mean writing an entire new book (or two). Here, we reiterate two principles that underlie the fundamental thinking of Chinese leadership.

Hierarchy is Key

Confucian teachings promote that "a minister should be loyal to his emperor, and a son should respect his father" (君臣父子 *junchen fuzi*). The strict yet subtle notion of hierarchy established by Confucius still exists. Such hierarchal order is even more obvious in the business world.

Due to the drastic changes brought on by China's recent economic reform, the social strata has undergone significant changes. New classes are emerging from the much simpler classes categorized in Mao's era. The nation used to be divided into three classes—workers, peasants, and intellectuals. Today, the most elite group, regarded as the "upper class," consists of senior government officials, acclaimed academics, entrepreneurs with assets worth over RMB 100 million (approximately US$12.5 million), international company executives, and SOE senior managers. They account for approximately 1 percent of the Chinese population. Power and wealth are the most important factors that distinguish a person's level of importance.

Leaders are Like Emperors and Parents

Within the Chinese business context, decision makers are viewed as "emperors," even more so in the SOE environment. The subordinates are "ministers" and are not meant to argue or disobey orders. The prevailing Confucian teachings endorse 忠 *zhong*—loyalty to one's emperor—which is much encouraged in the business community. We know of a case where a Chinese subordinate went to jail on behalf of the boss to show his loyalty.

However, there is also a saying that "working for an emperor is like being in the company of a tiger" 伴君如伴虎 *banjun ru banhu*, meaning such a position is so dangerous that one could lose one's life should the emperor turn in anger. Such fear often brings a enormous amount of politics into the organization. "Ministers" often spend more energy making sure that they are always "seen as loyal," rather than taking care of business.

Often a family culture exists in private enterprises and small companies. Respect for and obedience to parents, "filial piety" (孝 *xiao*), is a prerequisite to being an ideal person. Most business leaders do their best to duplicate the atmosphere of a "family" in the workplace, and treat their employees like children. The "parent" usually makes decisions, and again, no questions can or should be asked. Such a leadership style has a positive effect when the leader is a "kind parent" who makes the right decisions; the employees feel trusted and motivated, and the business expands accordingly. However, when the leader is dominant and strict, it usually creates a fearful atmosphere, and employees are criticized and punished without appropriate respect or communication.

Impact on Contemporary China

For two to three decades since the early 1950s, under the controlled-economy structure of Mao Zedong's era, China was run as a gigantic single economic entity. All businesses were owned, controlled, or funded by the government. There was no need for people to think, plan, lead, or manage a business in the pure commercial sense.

Becoming the party leader of an SOE was regarded as the most important and honorable career advancement. Most professional people, who excelled in their own positions (be it accountants, architects, or engineers), were invariably promoted to become leaders in charge of the Communist Party members at their workplace.

Today's Business Decision Makers

We all know that China has changed dramatically since the 1970s. However, old habits die hard. Most of today's managers, thirty-five years old and older, are still significantly influenced by that period.

There are a great number of successful Chinese leaders in all walks of life from the China region and its neighboring countries, including Taiwan, Hong Kong, Singapore, Malaysia, and Macao. In our analysis, we focused only on the Chinese from mainland China. We have seen that there are different approaches to leadership within different corporate structures depending on a leader's background and experience.

Witnessing History

Helen witnessed her father's rise in a local radio manufacturing factory in Tianjin. As he excelled at his job—he was of the earliest generation of electrical engineers—he was promoted and eventually became the Party secretary, the person who oversees the spreading of the Communist doctrine. He was moved from a highly technical job where he could contribute more to the business, to reading Communist documents and newspapers to his fellow factory workers for the rest of his working life. In SOEs today, the position of Party secretary is still the most important. Party secretaries rank above the president, chairman, or CEO and are the real decision makers of SOE businesses.

Helen's father considered the promotion a great honor. During her university years, he wrote to her with opening lines such as, "You know that the Party Congress has just issued a new document…" In many ways, he represents a typical passive, modest, and law-abiding Chinese citizen. He takes pride in doing his job to perfection and strictly abiding by the system.

Conclusion

The Chinese leadership qualities are built on traditional Chinese values that have a deep historical framework. International influence has started to garner increasing attention, particularly in the case of the next generation. However, for the majority, there is still room for change. A new form of leadership is required for Chinese leaders as they seek to globalize and blend the old with the new.

In the meantime, it is important for a Westerner to respect, understand, and learn about some of the traits of Chinese leadership. Without these true leaders, China would not have achieved what it has achieved to date.

As China emerges as the next world superpower, leaders who can successfully combine traditional Chinese wisdom and modern leadership knowledge from the West will come forth. They will be the ones to take their businesses to new heights globally, while those who refuse to change will struggle to grow and may eventually fade away, together with their businesses. We hope that you will find these new leaders to work with in China.

Chapter 5

Work Ethics

The more you do, the more likely you are to make mistakes
The Huainanzi [1]

Many centuries ago in China, a water bearer carried water from the stream in two large pots, each hung on the ends of a pole that he carried across his shoulders.

One pot had a crack in it, while the other pot was perfect and always delivered a full portion of water. At the end of the long walk from the stream to the house, the cracked pot was only half full. This went on every day for two years, with the bearer delivering only one-and-a-half pots of water. Of course, the perfect pot was proud of its accomplishments, perfect for the task it had been made for. But the cracked pot was ashamed of its own imperfection, miserable that it could accomplish only half of what it had been made to do.

After two years of what it perceived to be a bitter failure, one day, it spoke to the water bearer by the stream.

"I am ashamed of myself, because this crack in my side causes water to leak out all the way back to your house."

The bearer said to the pot, "Did you notice that there were flowers only on your side of the path, but not on the other pot's side? That's because I have always known about your flaw, and I planted flower seeds on your side of the path.

Every day while we walked back, you watered them. For two years, I have been able to pick these beautiful flowers to decorate the table. Without you being just the way you are, there would not be this beauty to grace the house."

In the international business community, the clash between traditional Chinese culture and Western business practices has surfaced as the main reason most Chinese operations of foreign companies suffer serious setbacks.

We are often asked to speak with the multinational teams. The expatriates don't understand why the Chinese think they are rude, opinionated, and that

---

[1] The *Huainanzi* 淮南子, also known as *Master(s) from Huainan*, is a collection of various philosophical treatises compiled under the mentorship of Liu An (179–122), Prince of Huainan. (*Encyclopedia of China,* 中國大百科全書, *Zhongguo wenxue* 中國文學, Vol 1: p. 275).

they do not respect their "face." They don't understand why their Chinese colleagues cannot or will not express their opinions or ideas in an open or transparent manner.

Many Chinese employees believe that the expats are "cracked pots." This chapter examines Chinese work ethics and explores why the Chinese are reluctant to take any initiative or be proactive—even though they are diligently watering the flowers day in, day out.

In general, the Chinese are hardworking, great team members, and can do a great job when the instructions are clear. However, when this is not the case, they are at a loss and will resort to a "do nothing" work ethic. They are reluctant to show initiative or express their real opinions, even when they harbor many.

Furthermore, they often interpret rules very differently. To them, interpreting the rules correctly is far more important than following them to the letter. Even though the rules may not change, their interpretation can change from day to day.

We explain why and how most Chinese employees follow the midstream philosophy. Maintaining an appropriate position at work can become their ultimate objective. This attitude, linked to the concept of 面子 *mianzi*, helps build a powerful network of connections—关系网 *guanxi wang*—around them. It is the constant nurturing and expanding of these networks that enable workers to move up the career ladder.

HISTORICAL CONTEXT

Under Mao Zedong's administration from 1949 to 1976, all businesses were state owned, controlled, or funded. Being a good employee meant conforming to instructions and doing as told. There was no need to think about the future or a career path. One simply had to be politically correct and follow orders without questioning. Being politically correct dominated most peoples' entire work life, especially during the late years of Mao's leadership.

During the Cultural Revolution (1968–1978), China, as a nation, plunged into a dark period and an entire generation of the workforce was forced to live as peasants. The majority of students from the urban regions were sent to the farming countryside to be "re-educated"—as were academics and all professionally trained people. The saying then was, "The more one knows, the more anti-revolutionary one becomes." Experienced and knowledgeable senior employees in their 50s and 60s almost vanished.

Some of our Chinese colleagues amusingly (and with some frustration) describe state-owned enterprises (SOEs) as tentacles of a giant octopus. The head is the Chinese government (in some cases, the central government; in others, city, regional, or district government departments). Managers are unable to take any actions without clear instructions or approval from the head, let alone the employees. Most of today's senior work force was either trained in or influenced by this SOE mentality.

Practices are changing rapidly, particularly in the non-SOE sectors. However, it is important to remember that SOEs are still the largest employers of China's 283 million urban workers.

Clearly, it is not just the non-Chinese who cannot understand what an SOE employee is thinking! Attempting to come to terms with these changes is a never-ending battle both within and outside China. It is worth noting that such thinking also exists, to some extent, in China's foreign and private businesses, as most of the experienced white-collar employees come from an SOE environment.

Traditionally, people with more skills prefer to work for foreign companies, mainly for their better financial benefits and career advancement opportunities.

The Government is Aware

The Chinese government openly admits that one of the key issues is that the vast number of SOE employees has difficulty adapting to change.

A report posted on the Ministry of Commerce website provides some insights. Note that some parts are typical Chinese government-speak (slogan-like and grand):

> "The planned economy has been replaced by the socialist market economy. This provides great energy and development space for China's modernization process... but the old mentality to which SOE employees are accustomed will not disappear automatically. For instance, the employees' mentality and behavior tend to be changeable, varied, diverse, and unpredictable. It becomes hard to guess what is really on their minds..."[2]

---

[2] Wei et al., "Reform Calls for Change of Mentality of SOE Employees," www.mofcom.gov.cn, (last accessed, May 2008).

Others made the change because they didn't have other options—their jobs were made redundant or they lost their jobs when the SOEs closed down or were sold off during the major restructuring of the early 2000s.

Overall, most Chinese employees realize that they need to change. They do their best to adapt to different cultures gradually, even though it is often quite difficult. Ongoing support from the new workplace, personal ambition, and the ability to change are critical success factors for this shift in mindset.

Cultural Context

Structures within organizations and within the Chinese society are equally influential on the mindset of Chinese employees. In China, hierarchy and a person's place are very important—everyone has his or her position within an organization and abides by orders diligently. When the most senior-ranking person is present at a meeting, no one will volunteer or contribute their opinions unless asked. A typical Chinese upbringing and education instills hierarchical obedience into most Chinese.

How is this hierarchal framework embedded in the Chinese mindset? We will take a closer look at the mainstream Chinese education system.

A System That Needs Reform

Apart from the small but growing number of private and international schools, the majority of Chinese students go through the public education system. Across China, most public schools offer the same subjects with centrally published and distributed textbooks.

Due to the vast number of students, the education system has been distorted to become a learn-by-rote and exam-focused one. A good student may obtain very good marks in exams and know the material very well, but may not necessarily understand the essence of the material, and may not acquire true knowledge.

A good schoolteacher is one who has the highest number of students admitted into higher education. The financial bonus for a high school teacher is usually linked to the number of students accepted by universities.

One Chinese parent Helen recently met described the system as efficient only in producing good students who will land good jobs (because they graduate from top universities). But the system does not teach the students how to be good at a job, or even live life more productively!

One thing the education system does well is to teach respect and obedience to authority. No one dares challenge the teacher, as he or she

What Is a Good Student?

While Helen was going through the education system in the mid-1970s, instead of "learning how to learn," she repeated after the teachers (rote learning) and memorized the textbook. While she may have sharpened her short-term memory, storing answers to questions that might be asked in exams, for a long period afterward, she had no interest in learning, and had seemingly lost the ability to think or listen to her own inner voice.

Yang Liu, a well-known young designer who runs her own business in Berlin, Germany, and Beijing shared her own experience with Helen. The daughter of an artist and an engineer, Yang is very bright and intelligent. Her design works have been widely exhibited in both the United States and Europe. She moved to Germany with her parents when she was thirteen.

Unlike Helen, she was rebellious all through her school years. When studying in Beijing, she constantly challenged the teachers and was punished accordingly. One punishment was to stand in a corner of the yard outside the classroom to reflect. She said there was no way she was going to be a good student. When asked how she was punished, she answered, "I think I stood in every single corner of the school!"

---

is the unquestionable authority on the subject. One does not question anything printed in the textbooks. And there is only one right answer to any question—the answer in print, endorsed by the teacher.

When a student shows initiative and questions a task, it is regarded as showing disrespect. After a few attempts, many Chinese quickly learn to behave in a certain way, within acceptable, clearly defined parameters—and they shy away from proactive thinking and action.

Those exceptional students who refuse to be molded into generic "good" students usually become very successful when they enter the workforce. In fact, most successful people in China weren't necessarily good students.

More on *Mianzi*: The Story of Ah Q

While the education system teaches respect and obedience to authority, there are other issues at play inside the Chinese mind. It is most humiliating for a Chinese to be criticized in front of his or her peers, worse when subordinates witness it. The real fear of becoming such a negative center of attention is to "lose *mianzi*."

Perhaps, the best-known Chinese writing about this is by Lu Xun (1881–1936), an eminent modern Chinese writer. One of his most famous short stories is titled *The True Story of Ah Q*,³ the chronicles of a peasant who views personal failure as success even up to his execution. The story, hailed as a masterpiece of modern Chinese literature, is still taught in Chinese schools. It is so well known that "Ah Q" has become the name for anyone who refuses to see the reality of failure.

The story traces the adventures of Ah Q, a peasant with little education and no regular work. He bullies the less fortunate, yet is fearful of those superior to him in rank, strength, or power. Ah Q is beaten and his hard-earned money is stolen. He then slaps himself on the face, and because he is the one doing the slapping, he sees himself as the victor of the misfortune.

The story concludes when Ah Q is arrested for a robbery he has not committed. When asked to sign a confession, he worries that he does not know how to write his name. The officers tell him to sign a circle instead. He focuses so completely on drawing a perfect circle that he does not realize that in doing so, it would be too late and he would be executed.

This story reveals Ah Q's extreme version of saving face and dramatizes the Chinese obsession with maintaining a good appearance in front of others.

However, it is important to not misread this story. The Chinese, in general, have mixed feelings about Ah Q. Most acknowledge that it is a brilliant portrayal of some bad elements in Chinese behavioral patterns, while also having good connotations. In the ongoing debates among the Chinese readers about Ah Q, some argue that he is a tragic coward who lived in a false reality. Some call people "Ah Q" when they look down on them, or when they want to shake some sense of reality into them. Others see Ah Q as the master of contentment. Some even recommend that parents put less pressure on their children, and adopt the "Ah Q spirit" to allow their children's emotional development.

Parents Are to be Revered

In addition to pressures at school, parental pressure contributes to a lack of initiative and independent thinking in Chinese employees.

It is important to look at the historical context. Until the mid-1980s, all employees were required to work full time, six days a week, with Sunday off. There were no annual holidays or extended maternity leave.

---

³ The most authentic English version published in China is *The True Story of Ah Q and Other Stories [1918–1926]*, translated by Yang Hsien-yi and Gladys Yang, (Foreign Languages Press, Peking, 1960, 1972).

Case Study: *Global TechCo: How Carl Saves His Face*

Tom and Helen arrived at the best spa hotel that Carl could arrange for in Kunshan. Frustrated, Tom explained to Helen that once again there was no schedule for the next few days. All Carl said was, "Come, and I'll arrange everything." (Chinese flexibility—frustrating as it may be.) Western executives are advised to "go with the flow," remain flexible, and do their best to accommodate important meetings and last-minute delays. On the other hand, when objectives cannot be met within a reasonable time frame, don't be afraid to cut the trip short.

To Helen's surprise, Carl turned up in khaki jeans and a LongChamp shirt. A good-looking friendly young man, somewhat emotional, he appeared almost too naive to fit the picture Helen had in her mind about him. Sitting in the tranquil café by the pool, Helen spent the rest of the day explaining repeatedly, in very clear Chinese, to Carl that Tom—not the founder—was the real decision maker, sharing that while the founder had founded the company, his ownership had been diluted to a very small percentage by the same group of venture capitalists that now control the company. As the CEO, Tom could either recommend the deal to the Board, or terminate it during his time in China.

Carl was genuinely shocked by the message. After being repeatedly told (in both English and Chinese) more than ten times, reality slowly sank in.

The next three hours at dinner were spent listening to Carl vent and complain that the deal would be greatly affected by the miscommunication. Then he finally began to focus on how to face his government contacts with the truth. Carl had to find a way out. Finally, he suggested that first, he would go alone to see Mr. Wang, one of the key people in the group, to "straighten things out." Given that the meeting with everyone was scheduled for the next morning, he had to leave right away.

Carl disappeared on a mission to sort things out—or so we thought.

At about 11:00 p.m., Helen's mobile rang. It was Carl's driver. He said that Carl had met with an accident and was being rushed to a hospital and that all meetings scheduled for the next day were cancelled.

Again, alarm bells went off. Was this the truth or a fabricated convenient incident? Helen discussed it with Tom, weighing the situation. To avoid more potential claims for compensation from Carl, Tom asked Helen not to disclose to Carl that he knew about the accident.

Helen's mobile rang again. The driver told Helen the name of the hospital and asked her to go there immediately.

By this time, it was almost midnight. Helen did not want to travel alone to the rescue of Carl. Perhaps it was best to leave him in the hospital to lick his wounds. If she went, he might attempt to compromise her, having the

(Continued)

(Continued)

opportunity to be with her without Tom. Both Tom and Helen doubted that an "accident" happened at such an opportune moment.

Helen called Carl, but his phone was switched off. She then called the driver to see how bad Carl's injuries were. The driver would not give her a straight answer and asked her to hold on while he went to find Carl. Next thing, he hung up the phone! Helen rang again, but his phone, too, was switched off.

By then, all alarm bells had sounded. Helen had heard of "accidents" like this that "conveniently" changed the course of business negotiations. The real question was whether or not Carl would stop here, or go one step further to make both Tom and her "unavailable" for tomorrow's meeting!

Tom and Helen exchanged many text messages in the following hour. (Tom did not want to use his room phone in case Carl chose to call him for help to "divide and conquer.") Helen suggested that they move to a hotel in Shanghai, to be in a bigger city and under less influence from Carl and his contacts. Tom agreed and suggested that they ring Carl's room in the morning before making the final decision.

As a result, grandparents looked after pre-school children, who barely saw their parents during the week. Usually, the grandparents did not discipline the children, and on the weekends, the parents would spoil them, often out of guilt about their absence.

However, when the children started school, they were immediately subjected to strict discipline and expectations. From "you could not do anything wrong," the implied message suddenly became "you cannot do anything right unless you are a good student." Parents did everything possible to get their children into good schools and demanded that they become excellent students. This stems from the teachings of Confucius. One of his sayings is that when a person excels in studying, he may become a government official 学而优则仕 *xue er you ze shi*.

Once at school, the Chinese children learn to respect and obey their parents as well as their teachers. Such authoritative status is established and unchallenged (for a very long time, if not forever). The rigid nature of the relationship with a parent, teacher, or master, and the depth of the respect for them are the pillars of Chinese societies.

Even though many parents encourage their children to treat them as equal friends, they don't want to see their authority challenged or undermined at all.

I Am Your Mother, NOT Your Friend

When Helen was a undergraduate student, a visiting lecturer from the United States told her that in the West, parents and children can be friends. They are free to talk to each other and share views and concerns.

She was excited to learn this and rang her mother later that evening. After hearing her excited words, her mother paused for a long time.

Then she replied in a very stern voice, "What in the world are you saying? What are they teaching you there? We are Chinese! Remember you are my daughter! Never ever think for once that I am your friend!"

From then on, Helen learned to not confide in her mother, and she has a rigid and structured relationship with her parents, common to many Chinese.

Chinese "Cracked Pots"

Unlike in the West, most Chinese parents do not tell their children how clever they are, or acknowledge individual achievements. Instead, parents tell children that they are never good enough. Even when they get full marks on school assignments, they are told that they should not rest on past glory. Modesty is a very important part of the Chinese character. The parents worry that if they compliment the children too much, they could become too proud.

Often the Chinese bring such modesty into their adulthood. There are occasions when Chinese job seekers will not acknowledge their own strengths and skills, even at job interviews. When asked what they think their strengths are, they will normally say, "I'm not really good at anything!" These are the "cracked pots" from the water bearer story.

For some Chinese, this treatment by their parents continues even after they start working. If they get a good job, say, at a foreign company, then their parents will keep repeating—"You must behave properly to hang on to such a good job"; "Only do what you're told, otherwise you'll be in trouble"; and "Listen carefully to your manager!"

Chinese managers and employees (ones with no international business exposure) will constantly seek approval—as their upbringing has resulted in a lack of self-confidence and a dearth of leadership skills. Seen through Western eyes, they often lack initiative (as they never learned or were never asked to exhibit this quality), will always ask for directions from authority (as they have been trained to do), and will blame someone else when they make a mistake (it was not their decision, so why should they be held responsible?).

CHINESE GENERATION Y

One group does not quite fit into the stereotypes we have described so far. Due to China's strong economic growth, some young Chinese Generation Y employees—the 25- to 35-year-olds (who make up about 50 percent of the current Chinese work force) have begun to show a different trait in their work ethics.

The good news is that they appear to be modernizing the traditional values, rather than simply Westernizing. Unlike the earlier generations, they do not unquestioningly accept hierarchies. However, responsibility for the extended family, adherence to 中庸 *zhong yong*—balance or harmony—as well as caring for their relationships still play a large role in their lives and thoughts. They want to take the initiative and share ideas, even though they may lack experience. They have high career expectations; and they also expect to work diligently to achieve these.

It is possible that some Chinese could misinterpret patriotism as arrogance, and go to the other extreme of "doing nothing" or "saying nothing," particularly when working in an international business environment. They think they know everything and refuse to be managed or

---

What Makes the Chinese Happy?

A survey asked, "If you could choose one thing to make your life happier, what would it be?" Over 80 percent chose to do something for their parents. One female interviewee answered, "I want my parents to have a beautiful house." Expecting that she would then think about herself, the follow-up question was, "If you already had that, what would be your second wish?" She thought about it for a while, and then said, "I'd like them to also have a fish pond in their garden."[4]

---

[4] Nandani Lynton and Kirsten Høgh Thøgersen, "Reckoning with Chinese Gen Y: New Research on Young Chinese Shows They Are Modernizing but Not Westernizing", http://www.businessweek.com/globalbiz/content/jan2010/gb20100125_065225.htm, (last accessed, March 2010).

> ### *Dare to Say No*
> Some of the Generation Y, however, have been indulged by always getting their way before they start working. Being "the only-child generation," some of them also lack the social skills to relate to others.
>
> We know a couple, Miranda and Cedric, as friends and neighbors. They own and operate a successful online health food business in Beijing. Miranda manages the business and recently told Helen this true story.
>
> She wanted to speak with the accountant, a "Generation Y" lady who had been newly recruited. She told the human resource manager to ask the accountant to come in to see her; however, the accountant did not do so. So Miranda went to the accountant's desk, and asked her if she could see her in her office.
>
> To this, the accountant replied, "No, can't you see I am busy?"

consider their work positions as insignificant. Often, they are opinionated, make many mistakes, and appear to think that they are too good for their jobs. This may become a growing trend as China progresses, and more and more people from this generation move into the workforce.

Chinese Work Ethics

To understand the Chinese work ethics, it is good to know the five most commonly followed rules by a Chinese employee:

Rule No 1: Do Not Make Mistakes

It is critical for a Chinese employee to make no mistakes while undertaking their assigned work. Often, they will choose to do nothing when instructions are not clear or when they find themselves in unfamiliar territory.

Rule No. 2: "The More You Do, the More Likely You Will Be to Make a Mistake"

This saying dates back almost 2,000 years. It has been passed along generations, hailed as an important attribute for being a sage 圣人 *shengren*, a term the Chinese use to describe an ideal human being.

It is important to remember that, in general, the Chinese strive to become sages by making fewer, or (even better) no mistakes in their lives. Translated into corporate behavior, it is only natural for the young female employee in the example below to wait for explicit orders. She was worried that had she

What Does Beautiful Mean?

Simone, a good friend of ours, works for a very large hospitality wholesaler headquartered in Germany. Their joint venture in China is quite successful. She occasionally travels to China and helps to organize exhibitions.

The last time we saw her in Beijing, after a major exhibition, she asked us to explain something. She said that in general, she was thrilled at how hard-working, cooperative, and brilliant the Chinese team was during the preparation stage of the exhibition. Everything was done perfectly according to her instructions.

However, during the exhibition, when she asked one of the girls to "keep the exhibition stand beautiful," she was very disappointed that she failed to perform such a simple task. She didn't water the flowers in the vase, so they withered; the floor was dirty, yet she never bothered to call the cleaner or do anything about it; the list went on and on.

She asked us, "Why is it so?"

---

interpreted the order herself, proactive action could cause criticism rather than encouragement.

To a Chinese employee, the instruction to "keep the stand beautiful" was far too vague. One needs to clarify instructions by giving clear and precise details and the measure of performance, that is, water the flowers twice a day, sweep the floor so it is clean at all times, smile at every visitor, and so on.

In the broader context, this simple rule should also apply to more complicated situations. A clearly defined office manual for a new employee, a performance guide for each job, a well mapped-out project plan detailing actions required and who is responsible for what task—all these will help in managing "typical" Chinese employees. Don't assume that your Chinese employees lack initiative—sometimes they hide it simply because they don't want to make mistakes!

Rule No. 3: Follow Orders

While Chinese employees will follow orders, they can also refuse an order in a "Chinese" way. This can be achieved without breaking or even bending the rules. In fact, it can be achieved by following the rules to the letter.

In the example below, a silent but effective protest was made by the staff to stay strictly within the rules—first, to show that they were "following the rules," and second, to demonstrate the inappropriate nature of the rule.

Protesting Against the Rules by Abiding by Them Religiously

A few years ago, Geoff consulted for a local service company in Beijing. For a while, there was no office manager and the small staff enjoyed a certain freedom outside the office routine while canvassing people across the city for marketing opportunities.

They were always out for meetings and having coffee in local coffee shops. However, when a new office manager was hired, he worried about the staff being out of the office and implemented a policy that unless he approved coffee breaks or client meetings, everyone had to stay at their desks.

Many months passed, then that manager left and another was appointed. Geoff, while working in the office, requested some assistance with a technical translation. The Internet was used to assist, but without the purchase of a dictionary, the translation could not be completed. After two weeks, it still had not been done.

The newly hired manager wondered what caused the delay. After much investigation, he was made aware of the old rule implemented by the old manager—no one was able to leave the office. In keeping with that rule, no one would go out of the office to buy the dictionary without approval!

Some of the senior employees in this example were ex-SOE employees. In a Western organization, one would expect the senior employees to voice their concerns about the restrictive work practices. In this organization, given the training and ethos of the senior employees, they chose a very SOE way of dealing with the problem.

In addition, the translation work was not regarded as part of any employee's "normal" duties. It was assigned to the staff as an extra job in addition to their daily tasks. They felt no urgency to complete the task. Not only was it not part of their job description, but also it was not a job to be done for the "big boss" (老板 lao ban)—the Chinese owner. In their eyes, completing such a task would not help advance their careers.

With all these implied rules and lack of initiative, how does an employee in the Chinese business environment achieve his or her career ambitions?

As Chinese leaders often manage their businesses on a "need to know" basis, information becomes key. Employees seek answers within the organization and strive to enhance their positions through greater knowledge of the business operation. They make use of their "connectedness" and form their own alliance groups and network with peers, subordinates, as well as superiors, who share a common interest.

Some of the smart, trusted, and informed longer-serving employees are favored by the leaders, who allow them to get a little more information. As they continue to perform and deliver benefits to the boss, they are taken in as eventual confidants. This, however, is usually a long, drawn-out process.

Rule No. 4: Get in (the Right) Line

For those without influence (political, family, or money), advancing their careers is achieved through this long drawn-out process of following a leader and aligning oneself with up-and-coming star performers.

This "follow the leader" process develops hierarchical structures. Ambitious workers will do their best to align themselves with a senior person with authority. Through this subtle and complex process of "queueing" (站队 *zhandui*), progress is made toward eventual leadership positions.

Understandably, it becomes crucial to get in the right line and ensure that your benefactor is performing above you.

Rule No. 5—The More You Do, the Worse It Gets

Both of us have worked as principals (owners), managers, consultants, and as employees in numerous Chinese organizations that are either foreign-funded and controlled, or are truly local and in no way related to the Western ideals of management and business structure.

Over time, we have witnessed Chinese work ethics in action, or one could possibly say "inaction." While one rule may be "the lesser you do, the safer you are," a similar rule applies to what one says in the business environment.

Chinese managers also enforce and protect their authoritative status through different means. While managers may not show their annoyance openly, the person who dares to challenge or show disrespect (even body language or a comment may cause such implications) will suffer the consequences after a meeting, quietly but effectively.

The mentality in the government civil servant sector was described as follows in a report:

> Chinese political culture is one that values seniority. Traditionally, young faces were not favored for key decision-making positions because they were considered too immature for leadership roles.
>
> Another perceived disadvantage of youthful officials has been their personal characteristics. More often than not, aspiring youths would not be trusted and promoted until they concealed or gave up what made them who they are.

That is why hopeful candidates for public offices usually choose to speak, behave, and even dress alike.[5]

A similar mentality exists in the business sector. Chinese employees worry about what their peers think about them and are always influenced by midstream thinking. The last thing they want is to be the center of attention (whether good or bad). Making a mistake is worse, as then they become the "target of public criticism" 众矢之的 *zhongshi zhidi*.

This rule has its benefits and negative impacts. On the one hand, it encourages an atmosphere of harmony, teamwork, and a sense of belonging. On the other hand, it emphasizes too much conformity by "doing the right thing"—often at the expense of showing initiative or taking responsibility for one's own actions.

Chinese Staff Meetings

When Geoff first came to live in China, he worked as the managing partner of an international legal partnership that had re-opened an office in Beijing. He had worked and lived in other parts of Asia, including Japan, but never in China. He had consulted with many Chinese foreign joint ventures but had spent little time managing Chinese employees. So, in the spirit of ensuring that his new staff knew what direction and opportunity existed in the rapidly growing office, he implemented his normal Monday morning meetings to bring everyone up-to-date with the developments in their office and other related international offices in the region.

The first meeting was a failure. The employees looked at him with blank faces and were clearly embarrassed to be there. The senior employees felt belittled being with the junior employees, and the junior employees felt awkward having to share a discussion with their immediate seniors. His first mistake was to mix different levels of management.

No one wanted to say anything or participate. It was a one-way gabfest headed by Geoff. After many meetings and frustrated attempts to elicit participation, he had to devise a way to relax the staff and assure them that there was no need to be embarrassed about asking silly questions. He also added a social aspect to the meetings.

Over time, the meeting atmosphere improved as Geoff insisted on a more communicative and open office culture, but it never reached the height of participation achieved in offices in other countries.

---

[5] "The New Young Leaders" (author unknown), *China Daily*, 26 January 2007.

However, the ambitious and smart workers master the art of positioning themselves by performing just well enough to get attention and trust from their influential superiors. By becoming "rising stars that are not too bright," they attach themselves to the conveyor belt of promotion the Chinese way.

Conclusion

In general, the Chinese do not want to or like to make any mistakes, even to the point of doing nothing. It may have much to do with both social conditioning and their career path.

A new hire with a long history in the SOE environment would be used to following a strict hierarchical structure. An employee with some foreign or international business experience will be more accustomed to the Western corporate culture, and more willing to be proactive and share his/her opinions. Employees with private sector experience, where the businesses are usually driven by profitability, will have different motivation from others. Private sector employees will support Western business interests when they see that working with them will contribute to their performance in the eyes of the owner or principal of the business.

In the meantime, with the much-promoted "going global" movement, an increasing number of Chinese companies are expanding overseas and hiring Western executives or employees. As the initiative gathers momentum, some of these work ethic issues will also surface within Chinese businesses.

The best corporate culture will nurture the employees in a balanced way—acknowledging personal pursuit as well as nurturing a sense of connectedness. Tomorrow's global employees are those who have mastered the art of combining Western professionalism with Chinese holistic thinking.

Chapter 6
How the Chinese Communicate

Tell people only one-third of what is on your mind
Zhou Xitao

The above saying is from a book compiled by Zhou from the Qing Dynasty (1616–1911). The book is a compilation of some anonymous yet popular sayings and quotes, and includes principles for people to live by and philosophies considered wise. The book has been widely followed and studied ever since. This particular saying is known to most Chinese, and many follow it as the golden rule of communication. The complete quote is, "When communicating with people, one should let them know only one-third of what is on one's mind, rather than telling the complete truth."

Let us consider below the Chinese brush painting. Note that the artist has left some space blank. Typical of most traditional Chinese paintings, this is done intentionally to enable the admirer to better appreciate the painting. The Chinese term for this is "leaving it white" (留白 liubai). Similarly, when it comes to communication, the Chinese prefer to leave some things unsaid for the listener to interprete.

One of the great frustrations for a foreigner in China is learning to understand the way the Chinese communicate. People unfamiliar with China and its culture must realize that the Chinese communicate in a completely different

Chinese brush painting

style. They are always very careful and share only a portion of what is on their mind.

There are "formal" and "informal" ways to convey meanings. There are meanings being conveyed without being spoken: A prime example is that the Chinese rarely say "no," even when that is what they think. The Chinese also communicate in many non-verbal ways, and sometimes, it is important to recognize who is speaking to understand the meaning.

Culturally, the Chinese hold indirect forms of communication in very high regard. Many Chinese poems and essays are admired because they excel in using language in such a way that the meaning is eloquently yet subtly expressed. Some Chinese love songs do not mention the word "love" but instead describe the feeling and use well-known analogies.

Throughout this chapter, we explain in detail, in both historical and cultural contexts, how and why the Chinese communicate in such different ways. Examples, including recent business cases, are used to better prepare the reader for the intricate and complicated Chinese style of communication. Some Chinese words related to communication are summarized for ease of reference. In the final section, we provide practical tools and guidelines to facilitate the communication process.

WHAT WE SAY ABOUT EACH OTHER

Many failed business ventures are a result of utter confusion between Western and Chinese counterparts. Western business people say the following:

- "We wasted so much time on these (Chinese) people. In the end, we realized they weren't interested from the very beginning! Why couldn't they just say 'no' at the first meeting?"
- "They told us there was no way our terms would work, so we gave up on them. But our competitor has just succeeded by engaging the Chinese! What is wrong with these people?"
- "The Chinese never gave us a clear indication of their opinion after all those meetings! We hardly spent time talking business. How can we tell what they are really saying?"

The Chinese business people say the following:

- "We don't understand why the negotiation has suddenly come to an end. We thought things were going so well! Sure they told us, 'no.' But we thought that was just a way to get us to agree with their terms."

- "We took these people (foreigners) out to banquets and looked after them so well. How is it that when it comes to talking business, they will not compromise, acting as if they don't know us at all?"
- "They told us many things that we simply cannot comprehend or want to believe—all we really wanted to know was whether or not they were going to start working with us."

How can there be such profound misunderstanding? Are the Chinese ambiguous by nature? Are they lying? Why is it that even when the Chinese speak English and the Westerners understand every word, they still don't know what's been said?

Important Chinese Communication Terms

The following are some important terms and words used in Chinese communication.

Formal and Informal Terms

In the Chinese context, people speak formally and informally. Informal talk is often used when the Chinese are at home, with close friends, and at places where they feel safe and trusted. Under such circumstances, a Chinese person will typically let his/her guard down and speak frankly.

However, on formal occasions, formal language is put to use. Often, a Chinese person will speak as little or as vaguely as possible when asked for a definite opinion or feedback, even more so when he/she is not the most senior person there.

When the occasion calls for a speech, the Chinese often talk in 套话 *taohua* and 空话 *konghua*, superficial or meaningless talk, or 大话 *dahua*, exaggerated statements, or even 假话 *jiahua*, false statements. However, in certain regions and industries where people are less exposed to the Western business community, and especially among the state-owned enterprise (SOE) managers, you may encounter the extreme example of *taohua*—superficial, meaningless Chinese "weather talk." Among these groups, status and the Chinese view of hierarchy and leadership can prevent frank discussions.

The Chinese speak formally during meetings. In other words, they may talk about the weather, the growth of the Chinese economy, or their company; however, what they are really saying is something else—which can be totally unrelated. It is only after they become very comfortable with you as friends that they switch to "informal" language, which reveals a lot more about intentions.

A Very "Chinese" Meeting

Helen attended a meeting in which a European client explored joint venture opportunities with a large regional SOE. The SOE general manager (GM) turned up with ten people, significantly outnumbering Helen and her client. He then gave a welcome speech that gave them a full review of the government policy changes since the economic reform, from Deng Xiaoping to the current leader, saying how wonderful it was that only because of all these could he meet such distinguished guests like them. That speech alone took twenty minutes!

After the meeting was finally concluded two hours later (during which the Chinese GM spoke most of the time), the European executive asked Helen, "What exactly is he saying?" She explained to him that most of the speech was *taohua* (weather talk). By keeping the talk superficial, he was actually conveying the message that he would like to be invited to Europe for a visit (and some sightseeing) before discussing details about the joint venture. However, with all the subordinates present at the very first meeting, that was the only suitable way of delivering the real (and well hidden) message.

Communication Tip—太极 *tai chi* talk

When dealing with a Chinese person in a business setting, especially in the very early stages of a relationship, it is critical to remember that the Chinese do not get straight to the point. They prefer to talk about "formal" things. They might just touch on sensitive key topics to get a feel of what you are thinking. Some Chinese perfect this skill to an art form. A Chinese phrase describes such circular talk as 太极 *tai chi* talk.

As more and more people have now been exposed to Western culture and business practices, a growing number of successful Chinese business people have mastered a more direct way of communication. They will ask, "What can we do for you?" right after the rituals of shaking hands and taking photos. When you raise a question or state the purpose of your meeting, they are usually quite frank and open in their answers, and don't waste your time and energy further.

"White Talk" (白说 *Baishuo*)

Besides *liubai*, there are more Chinese words related to "white" that are handy to know. For example, "white" (白 *bai*) not only means the color white, but also that a certain action is in vain; "white waste" (白费 *baifei*) means that the effort is in vain; "white food" (白食 *baishi*) means a free meal; "eat white food" (吃白食 *chi baishi*) means to eat a meal without working for it. White talk (白说 *baishuo*) means that a person has wasted all his words without achieving the goal. It is used to describe a situation where someone fails to persuade. Another useful Chinese word to remember is 客气话 keqihua, which means a polite offering that implies nothing. For example, the Chinese will say, "Come and visit us at our house when you have time," but you need to follow up to check whether they really mean it or are just being polite (客气 keqi).

Leave Some Things Unsaid

Liubai, as an artistic term, describes the Chinese traditional painting referred to earlier in this chapter. The same logic applies when the Chinese communicate. They sometimes leave things unsaid, so that the listener can ponder on the implied message. Often, what is "not said" can be as important as, if not more so than, what is actually said.

Bill Gates Comes to China

When Bill Gates visited China for the third time in 2003, he met again with the then President Jiang Zemin. The meeting went on for 45 minutes longer than scheduled. During the entire meeting, only ten minutes were spent discussing the progress of Microsoft's business—the rest of the time, topics ranged from family to the financial market to the performance of Microsoft stock.

Communication Tip—essential white talk

During business negotiation, it is common for much of the conversation to be made up of "white talk" and *keqihua*. While not considered part of the real content, it is still very important in the Chinese context. The Chinese never see that as a waste of time. Not only are these conversations considered

An "International" Conference?

In 2005, we were engaged by a government logistics association in China to assist with planning and marketing a high-level global conference for 300 people. Designed to be the first important and comprehensive conference focusing on all major logistics businesses in China, the intent was to form an executive-level platform for China and the Western logistics industry leaders. The association was to ensure that all related Chinese government and business leaders would support and attend the conference. The head of the association repeatedly expressed his strong wish of running an "international" conference.

(Continued)

(*Continued*)

So our team conducted research (with our international contacts in the industry) to identify what would be a truly successful strategy to organize such a conference. We created a very professional agenda with both local and international speakers, and marketed the event through various foreign chambers of commerce in Beijing as well as through overseas partners.

Clash between teams

Then things started to go wrong. The Chinese association criticized us for spending too much time and money promoting the event internationally. The team was too expensive (we hired expatriate professionals) and the venue, too fancy. They didn't agree with our promotional material design and insisted that their printer could design and print the material as they had done for many previous conferences. We could not tell them that perhaps that was why the promotion was not internationally successful in previous years!

We were frustrated, as the association could not market the conference to key Chinese government and business leaders effectively. We then had to take over the domestic marketing for the sake of a quality conference. However, as the list of issues kept increasing, we lost two months of critical time putting everything together. The commercial viability became such a concern that we suggested to the association that they postpone the conference.

They refused, as doing so would mean "losing face." The head of the association said that in the past, he was able to organize a conference within a week! We had to make an immediate decision to stop financing the project but still supported them in bringing some overseas guests and local expatriates who were interested in attending.

What "international" really meant

The association was very satisfied with the outcome of the conference! They were thrilled that it was the first time that they had so many foreign delegates. Only then did we realize what the head of association meant by "international" in the first place—he meant that he wanted some foreigners attending his (very Chinese) conference! We could have done that without doing any of the hard work (or investing our hard cash)!

essential in relationship building, they also serve as "testers" to get a feel of you and your intentions. Westerners need to make allowance for the seemingly aimless discussions about irrelevant topics and participate with genuine enthusiasm. As aimless as the topics may seem, they can serve a special purpose.

SEVEN REASONS THE CHINESE COMMUNICATE DIFFERENTLY

Throughout their lives, the Chinese learn to master the art of ambiguity, balancing the 阴 *yin* and 阴 *yang*. Most of the Chinese one encounters in China will be highly skilled in this art and will neither be able to break free from the habit nor be willing to open up when talking to the non-Chinese.

No. 1: Multi-layered Communication

The Chinese communicate in a high-context, multi-layered manner. Not only is this mode of communication highly regulated in social settings, it is also rather prevalent in the commercial and political environment. Therefore, to effectively communicate with the Chinese, besides what you hear, it is also equally important to have an understanding of the overall context.

For example, when a Chinese is talking, he or she will intuitively take into account the circumstances. Is this a formal meeting or a casual gathering? Is this location a meeting room, a restaurant, or someone's home? With whom am I speaking? Is he or she more senior or junior in status? Is he or she a colleague? What are the social considerations? What is the topic (political issues or national concerns)? What is the intent? Is the purpose enhancing or building relationships, or achieving a clearly defined outcome, say signing a contract or securing a job opportunity?

No. 2: Strong Hierarchical Framework

China's hierarchy is diligently followed by everyone, even more so in the business context. For example, in a structured meeting environment,

Case Study: *Global TechCo's Long March*

> Let's revisit a small detail in this case. On several occasions, Tom asked Carl how much he wanted to be paid for his introductions and efforts. Carl repeatedly said he wanted no financial rewards. Then he turned 180 degrees to demand more than what would be regarded commercially reasonable. Unfortunately, not only was it too late, but it also created doubt in the relationship and made him lose credibility. Why did Carl behave in such a manner?

the Chinese believe that one should speak only under the following conditions:

- When one is the most senior person present.
- Only when asked by a superior when one is not the most senior.
- When what one says is absolutely necessary.

In a formal meeting with a group of Chinese, most of the time, only the most senior person will talk and answer questions. The others will not speak unless asked to do so by that senior person. When you involve a group member in the discussion by asking a question, he or she will answer only should the senior person agree. Therefore, to ensure the best use of your time and that of the others, no questions or topics should be directed to the less senior people. Failing to appreciate such protocols may cause unnecessary damage to the relationship, as the most senior-ranking Chinese may see you as being disrespectful of his or her authority.

Things are different when the less senior-ranking Chinese are asked to speak by their senior colleagues. Often, they will talk but only very briefly.

No. 3: Culturally Speaking

A person who is opinionated or talks a lot is regarded as arrogant, ignorant, or lacking in respect for others. Popular sayings are "silence is gold" 沉默是金 *chenmo shijin* and "the more you speak, the more likely you are to say something wrong" 言多语失 *yanduo yushi*.

However, it is also a tradition in China that during meetings, there should not be too much silence, which could be embarrassing for the guests. To fill in the spaces and relieve the sense of awkwardness, usually the most senior person will usually say something or ask someone else to talk. In the latter case, he or she will usually define a topic (usually of no real importance) for the subordinate to speak about, then cut in when he or she wants to speak.

No. 4: Inward-looking Nature

Chinese holistic thinking and the training for writing and reading Chinese fosters an inward-looking culture. The Chinese believe that the ideal world is a harmonious and peaceful society where everyone finds his or her contentment among others and with nature. Most Chinese are gentle and obedient. As we know, the Chinese invented gunpowder to perfect the art of fireworks—not for weaponry. It did not occur to them to use it as a tool to invade other nations.

Throughout history, China has been happy to trade with the rest of the world in a peaceful manner. Philosophers and scholars left behind volumes of teachings advising people to reflect upon themselves, saying self-development and self-discipline are the best way to cultivate and reach enlightenment. One of the most prevailing spiritual pursuits, Buddhism, promotes being emotionless as an ideal state. It is regarded as the ultimate achievement for a Chinese to conceal his or her feelings.

A manifestation of this inward-looking emphasis is the traditional Chinese greeting—folding one's hands together and bowing to the others. There is no touching involved as in the Western way of greetings—no shaking hands, hugging, or kissing.

For generations, the Chinese have believed that a mature and accomplished person should be humble, reserved, and quiet. Many Chinese today still spend most of their lives perfecting the art of putting on a façade so no one can guess what they are really thinking or feeling. No one can really get inside their minds. The relevant saying is, "One should never show one's true feelings on one's face" 喜怒不形于色 *xinu buxing yuse*.

No. 5: It is All About "Face" (面子 *mianzi*)

We have been asked many times why it is that the Chinese will never say no. Our view is that the Chinese do say no, but in their own way (sometimes even by saying yes!).

We reiterate that protecting one's own and other peoples' *mianzi* (face) is regarded as the most important thing in China. The manifestations are far reaching. The Chinese believe that saying "no" to someone will make the other person lose "face"—the ultimate expression of disrespect.

Over the years, the Chinese have perfected many ways to convey the meaning of "no" without damaging the other person's *mianzi*. In business meetings, when they have a different opinion, they will always start their sentence with, "I agree with what you said, but…" or "You have made an excellent point, however…" They are not lying, or making false statements (假话 *jiahua*) but are showing respect and maintaining a friendly atmosphere so that the meeting can go on without confrontation. "We agree to disagree" is not a popular concept in China!

Even when the Chinese are not interested in a business proposal, they will not refuse it outright because they don't want to disappoint the other party. They are concerned that a refusal would be interpreted as "We don't like your proposal, therefore we don't like you." They will normally say, "That sounds very interesting," or "We shall discuss this among ourselves later."

> ### Case Study: *Global TechCo's Long March, Day 3*
>
> Helen and our friend Tom, as you recall, were facing a delicate situation where Carl, their Chinese contact, had an alleged car accident. Surprisingly, when Helen rang Carl's room the next morning, Carl answered the phone, in a barely audible voice. Tom and Helen cautiously made plans to meet him personally. Carl was in his hotel room, propped up in bed with a big painful expression on his face. Boxes of both Western and Chinese medicines and an X-ray photo lay by his side.
>
> He said that the hospital was too dirty and noisy so he asked to be sent back to the hotel last night. Luckily, there were no broken bones, just some ruptured skin where the seat belt was. However, the car was completely written off (and of course nowhere to be seen).
>
> Then, with a frown and a painful experssion, he said that the meeting last night, however, had gone well. He managed to explain the situation to Mr. Wang, the co-investor, who said he'd come to the hotel to meet Tom. (However, he prevented Mr. Hu, the key investor, and the government contact from meeting Tom directly.)
>
> Later that morning, a brief meeting was held next to Carl's bed with Mr. Wang and his assistant. Mr. Wang is what the Chinese call a "grassroots" entrepreneur. He grew up in a little country village, had no higher education, and made his fortune by converting his early business contacts into opportunities with perfect timing. His group now owned properties, an eco-vegetable garden, a logistics company, and a trading company. However, he had neither dealt with foreigners nor had he been involved in a foreign acquisition or investment before.
>
> After listening to Tom, who set everything straight about how far away the technology was from commercialization (the founder had made overly optimistic promises a few years ahead of reality), Mr. Wang proposed a totally different structure instead of the total buyout offer. What he proposed was a conservative joint venture, using his property, Global TechCo's technology and cash as a base, then using these to leverage government funding. Both sides agreed to further discussion the next day.

No. 6: Internal Censor Mechanism

It is important to appreciate that before a Chinese person speaks, he or she will go through an "internal filtering/censor mechanism" that has developed over many years. Throughout a Chinese person's childhood, schooling, and early employment, they learn to bite their tongues and follow strict protocols and hierarchical order. Their cultural and educational influences serve to create people who will reserve their views or feelings, and will say only a portion of what they really think.

Things a Chinese person has been taught to consider before speaking include

- say only "politically correct" things—to say otherwise means trouble;
- speak only when asked to do so by a superior;
- never speak too much, as one may be regarded as being too proud, disrespectful, or arrogant, and one's remarks could be turned against oneself;
- show respect by listening more than talking;
- when there are decision makers present, never speak without approval;
- don't comment until a general consensus is reached (don't become the beam that sticks out); and
- remain emotionless (no facial expressions, body language, or verbal statements) as it is regarded as a sign of professional conduct.

No. 7: Trained to Listen to the "Unsaid"

Chinese culture emphasizes that what is unsaid is actually more important than what is said—"It is all said in the unsaid" 一切尽在不言中 *yiqie jinzai bu yan zhong*. Another saying—"One should listen to the tone rather than what is being said" 听话听音 *tinghua tingyin*—means that the same words can be used in a different context, said in certain tones, or presented in certain ways that result in completely different meanings or indications. The subtle difference means that the listener must pay close attention to what is being communicated, both verbally and physically.

A Chicken Tries to Speak to a Duck

A high-profile dispute surrounding Danone (a French food conglomerate) and Wahaha (the largest beverage, yogurt, and dairy producer in China) demonstrates how different styles of communication can escalate problems to much larger proportions and bring damages beyond measure.

For more than eleven years, the joint venture was regarded as a "match made in heaven." With financial support from Danone, Wahaha grew its sales from less than €100 million in 1996 to over €1.8 billion in 2006. Danone enjoyed handsome financial rewards (in 2006, China contributed €10 million to its group revenue, accounting for 10 percent of its total revenue). The original investment was US$43 million dollars for a 51 percent share of five joint ventures that grew to more than forty.

(Continued)

(*Continued*)

However, a two and half year dispute between the two parties and dueling lawsuits filed in courts around the world clearly show that there were long-standing problems that needed attention. Wahaha's long-time chairman, Zong Qinghou, admitted to the Chinese media that, "I was simply putting up with lot of things, hoping they would go away." Instead of communicating with his French partner when there was a need to do so, he did it the "Chinese way" by going around the problems. At the beginning of the bitter dispute, Danone seemed to be shocked by the miscommunication. One of the managers in the joint venture lamented that Emmanuel Faber (Chairman of the Group Joint Venture on behalf of Danone) did not know half of the forty CEOs that ran their joint ventures.

An article in the *International Herald Tribune*, June 2, 2007, reported that an internal investigation begun two years previously by Danone had blown up into a brawl that not only threatens the joint venture but also the reputation of both the Chinese group and the French group in the eyes of the global business community.

It began in 2005, when executives at Groupe Danone noticed something peculiar in the financial figures coming from China.

After a lengthy investigation, Danone officials concluded that their closest partner in China, Zong Qinghou, was operating secret companies outside the joint venture—companies that were mimicking the joint venture and siphoning off millions of dollars.

In August 2007—after months of negotiation between Danone and Zong failed to resolve the dispute over those companies and the ownership of the Wahaha brand—Danone filed a lawsuit in California against a company controlled by Zong's relatives. That lawsuit intensified the quarrel between Danone and its Chinese partner into a nasty, and at times bizarre, battle for control. The leaders of China and France even addressed the dispute at the 2007 presidential summit.

It is also revealing that, throughout the dispute, Danone (via their PR agency Ogilvy Shanghai) focused on their legal rights and how Zong's action had breached the agreement and damaged shareholder value, while Zong claimed that Danone was trying to "steal away" a well-known Chinese brand and that all the accusations were false. He even called for government support to "save a national brand."

One Chinese journalist described the dispute as, "a chicken trying to speak to a duck" (鸡同鸭讲 *jitong yajiang*)—both Danone and Zong are speaking in their own languages.

Remarkably, we found that most of the Chinese and Western media have been unbiased when following the dispute. Some Chinese bloggers even called for Zong to stop linking his commercial dispute with Danone and "national pride," warning that this could damage the reputation of the entire Chinese business community.

By September 2009, the two parties jointly announced a settlement for Wahaha to buy back the 51 percent share Danone had in the existing joint ventures, thus ending all legal proceedings related to the dispute. According to Professor Teng Bingsheng at the Cheung Kong Graduate School of Business in Beijing, deep distrust and loss of face on both sides had led what was once "one of the most successful alliances in China" into a "case study" of un-sustainable relationships.

TIP Communication Tip—read body language

Reading body language will not only give you a clearer picture of what is really happening but also will assist you to know who is making the decisions and how well the meeting is proceeding.

Geoff has professional legal training and was educated in the traditional Western way. It was re-education for him during his stay in China where he was not able to communicate directly using his well-honed language skills. Being generally argumentative by nature (and training), he was at times confused and frustrated that he could not deal directly with the "unsaid."

However, over time, he started to develop "body language skills" that helped him understand the underlying meanings in many meetings. Body language is an excellent gauge for how things are proceeding, even when one lacks an understanding of what is being discussed verbally (subtly or otherwise).

Too much focus on the unsaid

Westerners need to be careful with even the most trivial of things. Geoff recently asked a secretary in his office to buy some stationery they urgently needed, and to ring if there was a problem. But Geoff also said that she could buy things that were needed in the office even if they were not on the list.

After twenty minutes, she rang to ask about all kinds of things. Geoff told her to use her discretion to buy the needed items and that it was not necessary to call constantly. What Geoff suddenly realized was that she had interpreted his unsaid message as, "Ring when there is a problem and don't buy anything else unless you have my permission!"

Implied Rules That The Chinese Follow

Communication can be so difficult and complicated that even the Chinese themselves have trouble with it! However, there are implied rules, which we reveal here.

No. 1: Show Your Face

The Chinese believe that relationships (or connections, 关系 *guanxi*) are built over a long time. Therefore, establishing a trusted business relationship involves a series of meetings, banquets, and other networking activities to facilitate communication and the bonding process.

These activities can cover a whole array of standard Western bonding techniques (drinking, eating at restaurants, playing golf or tennis) and also involve some clearly China-centric activities such as foot massages and spa sessions.

In recent years, very elaborate 24/7 spa centers have opened across China, which include spa and bathing facilities. After having enjoyed the spa experience, everyone wears the pajamas provided and proceeds to another section of the spa center where they can mingle and enjoy all-you-can-eat smorgasbords, play ping-pong, cards, and mahjong, watch huge plasma TVs, surf the Internet, and play online games. Other quieter rooms provide relaxing foot and body massages.

The Chinese regard going to a spa together as another form of "business meetings." Spas provide a comfortable, family environment, and the Chinese believe they are a good place to get to know one another. The atmosphere creates equality—where everyone even wears the same pajamas! All outside trappings and wealth are left outside the door. Conversations, therefore, are more direct and revealing.

🛈 Communication Tip—be there or be square

The Chinese prefer face-to-face meetings to any other form of communication. Faxes, telephone calls, and emails are not to be used as primary tools when establishing a key relationship or negotiating with the Chinese. You need to make the effort to show up personally, and spend as much time as possible bonding with your Chinese counterparts.

As the relationship grows and the business dealings are developed, you can use remote telecommunication tools to sort out the logistics. However, it must be remembered that your presence is the most important factor in any successful and effective relationship.

No. 2: Leave the Best First Impression

Malcolm Gladwell's book *Blink* examines the importance of first impressions and rapid cognition, reflecting on the thoughts that occur in the blink of an eye. When you meet someone for the first time, or walk into a house you are thinking of buying, or read the first few sentences of a book, your mind takes about two seconds to jump to a series of conclusions, even when those conclusions are later modified by other experiences.

First impressions are significant for everyone; yet they may mean even more to the Chinese—"right brain" thinkers, who are more visually oriented, and more attuned to the "blink" phenomenon. When meeting a Chinese person for the first time, be aware of the impression you make. It is important. While emphasis can be on the personal—how you dress and conduct yourself—much revolves around how you present your business. If you do not speak Chinese and need a translator, the translator's presentation should reflect your business in ways beyond the comprehension of a foreigner new to China. In general, the Chinese expect glossy brochures and artistically prepared business cards. Small but elegant corporate gifts from your home country (preferably not made in China) are much appreciated.

No. 3: Engage the Best Interpreter

Communicating in a different language can be difficult, even more so when it is all through a translator. It is vital to choose the most appropriate person. The best linguistic scholar can be your worst translator, if he or she does not understand the business motives or culture of your own corporation, or has no fundamental knowledge about your Chinese counterpart.

And it's not just words that need to be translated. Knowledge of the background and culture of your Chinese hosts is often such a vital factor that it can make or break your plans. Too often, negotiations fail due to misinterpretation by or ignorance on the part of the translator. Being bilingual (or multi-lingual for that matter) does not mean that the translator will understand what is truly being discussed.

Therefore, choose your translator very carefully. Just because a person speaks Mandarin or a suitable dialect does not mean they are the best translators. Remember, China is like America with diverse cultures.

A thorough understanding of both cultures, a proper brief by you (about the purpose of the meeting as well as anything else that is relevant), and some homework about the Chinese party, the local players in your industry, as well as other foreign competitors are essential elements to ensure smooth communication and mutual understanding.

Even when your Chinese business counterparts speak English with you, it is normal for them to leave some things unsaid for the listener to ponder over. Remember also that what you say may not be what the Chinese hear, as they always intuitively listen to the unsaid.

One should ask the interpreter to not only verbally translate what is being said but also to elaborate on the underlying intentions, or as much as the interpreter can "get." If possible, it is best to have an in-house person perform this seemingly unimportant role. Hiring an in-house translator will provide some consistency and comfort in the eyes of the Chinese, as it says that you are prepared to be in China for a long time.

Ideally, your translator should also have corporate or managerial experience in your true business as it is vital for him or her to convey your true business intent or motives. A translator must not just translate your words but also appreciate the context and business background of your corporation.

Best and Worst Translators

Geoff hired a Hong-Kong-born translator who had spent a considerable amount of time overseas. Most of Geoff's business was conducted in northern China, and the translator's Hong Kong Mandarin accent and arrogant mannerisms (unfortunately, some older Hong Kong Chinese can be condescending toward mainland Chinese) meant the faltering of many business meetings with the local Chinese. At the time, Geoff had no idea how disastrous it was to have that person as a translator!

One of the best translators Geoff hired was trained in business but also had excellent linguistic skills. This is an unusual mix. Many linguistically gifted people are neither business-minded nor focused on what their clients wish to achieve.

After traveling in China with Geoff's team for a few days, the translator began to conduct the meetings and say things during the meetings even before Geoff was able to express the same view in English. In fact, she began to talk on issues that had previously been covered and made the meetings more efficient and effective. Obviously, you do not want a translator to take over the meetings (which can happen), but with de-briefing sessions and her ability to understand the business, Geoff's translator became an extremely valuable asset.

🅣🅘🅟 Communication Tip—find a competent local translator

Many international companies use Chinese translators from the southern part of China to conduct business in the north. This can be a costly mistake. There are long-standing cultural differences between regions in China and deep-rooted prejudices exist between ethnic groups. To have a culturally unacceptable person translating for you can greatly affect your communication, and more importantly, your outcomes.

Remember that translators reflect your business and its attitude toward the people you are doing your best to impress. If you don't have a large enough operation in China to engage an in-house translator, it is best to identify a professional translator based in the region you are visiting via referral from your local Chinese operation or network. For those who have not yet established such contacts, your embassy, trade associations, or Chambers of Commerce are appropriate avenues to start with.

Once you find the most appropriate translator, do not hesitate to ask questions to clarify critical or important issues, and verify what you have heard when necessary. When appropriate, at the end of the meeting, summarize

Don't Talk Me Down

A few years ago, Helen was working with an Australian management consulting firm on a potential project in Shanghai. The client was a large Chinese–German joint venture in the car industry. The firm's managing director had conducted a series of promising meetings with both the Chinese and the German managers. This meeting was Helen's first, and was the one meant to "seal the contract."

Shortly after the "real discussions" started, Helen noticed that the client's interpreter started to "tone down" what was being said. Serious issues that were pointed out to the client were reduced to small "imperfections." Instead of translating exactly what was being said so that the client would realize how much help they needed from the consulting firm, the interpreter appeared to be more concerned about her own job. She used words such as "maybe," "perhaps," and "we seem to think" to weaken the firm's findings and recommendations, in order to deliver the message in a polite way to her superiors. Fortunately, the conversation was conducted in English (with the interpreter translating for the client's Chinese managers) so Helen was able to intervene and take over the discussion.

the main points discussed together with the Chinese counterparts to ensure common understanding and agreement by all parties present.

Should you encounter a similar situation to the one mentioned in the example "Don't Talk Me Down," such misrepresentations must be stopped as early as possible. When possible, have a trusted Chinese person present who can alert you to such distortions, even though he or she is not the official interpreter.

However, things can get a bit out of hand even when you do your best to avoid miscommunication. Understandably, giving face and receiving face is an essential element of communication in China, but at this point, we must clarify that face does not necessarily mean manners.

According to the Chinese, when someone is higher than you on the social or business stratum, their rudeness can be tolerated. However, this only works in one direction. Rudeness to someone above you in any hierarchy is never tolerated. So you need to devise other ways to communicate your message. See the following example.

No. 4: Keep Some Thoughts to Yourself

When communicating with the Chinese, do your best to listen to the unsaid message. Suppress the urge to interpret messages at face value. Observe body language; do your best to see the "big picture." In the meantime, be mindful that the Chinese will be listening to your unsaid message, even when there isn't one!

There Must Be a Way Around This

Roger, our senior expatriate friend, has been working in China for more than two years. He has just started to develop sufficient patience to maintain his composure and conduct business effectively in China.

He heads the China operation of a company that sells large-scale equipment to major local companies. One order can be worth millions of dollars. At a recent meeting, he was seeing a long-standing customer in the hope of selling more heavy equipment in the context of a booming market.

The senior Chinese negotiator for the buyer started the meeting with a tirade of abuse and ranted for twenty minutes—telling our friend about problems in a scathing and unsavory (by any standards) manner. Our friend simply sat opposite, accepting the abuse and letting it roll over him.

The natural reaction was to argue and dish out his own abuse to the senior Chinese, which would have made him lose face, and would have potentially destroyed the long-standing relationship. However, our friend waited for the tirade to cease and asked the translator to translate his reply—line by line (an effective way to avoid the translator softening or skewing the message):

- We have been in a long-term relationship for many years (translate).
- This relationship is deeply cherished by the supplier (translate).
- It is now like a marriage that has gone a bit sour (translate).
- At this point, you seem to have left the large bed and gone to sleep in a separate bedroom (translate).
- I want to know what I can do to make sure we can get back into the big bed together (translate).

The entire Chinese buyer team started laughing. Instantly, their mood changed, became constructive, and solutions were soon found. Note that the issues raised by the Chinese buyer were never confronted head on, and instead, were dealt with sensitively and warmly, seeking conciliation, not confrontation. We salute our friend who has learnt so much in China!

Remember, when a Western person speaks 100 percent of what is on his or her mind, a Chinese person shares and responds with only a portion of what's inside theirs. This leads to countless misunderstandings. Though Westerners may take pride in being transparent and talking frankly, the Chinese will still think they are hiding something—or perhaps that the Westerners are just plain crazy!

No 5: Common Sense Still Prevails

As ambiguous as the Chinese can be, when one pays enough attention and asks the right questions, one can and will discern what is really being said. There are many competent professionals who can help when it comes to understanding and dealing with the Chinese business culture.

However, a word of warning: Do not follow all the advice too literally. Apply common sense and sound business judgment. Be confident in what you have to offer and trust that the Chinese will appreciate your integrity and professionalism. Most will be tolerant and forgiving of miscommunications as long as you show that your intentions are good, and that you are genuine about what you are communicating. As China continues its amazing journey toward globalization, many Chinese business people will begin to understand more about where you are coming from and your attitudes toward international business.

CONCLUSION

When communicating with the Chinese, let go of the Western ways of communication, be open minded, and examine where the Chinese are coming from. Remember, too much information can be no different from no information as far as the Chinese are concerned. The Chinese may think you are lying when you share 100 percent of what is on your mind, as their norm is to withhold a certain percentage.

Ask questions. Respect the Chinese way and always listen attentively. Do not hesitate to ask questions to clarify vital or important issues, and verify what you have heard. When appropriate, summarize the main points discussed to ensure common understanding and agreement at the end of the meeting.

Always listen to the unsaid message—observe body language, seek the big picture like the Chinese do all the time, and when possible, find someone who understands both languages, both cultures, AND your business to help decipher the true message delivered by the Chinese.

In summary, the Chinese communication tips are as follows:

No. 1: Tai Chi Talk
The Chinese do not get straight to the point. They prefer instead to talk about formal matters. They might just touch upon sensitive key topics to get a feel of what you're thinking. Some Chinese people perfect such skills to an art form.

No. 2: Essential White Talk
It is common for much of a business conversation to be made up of "white talk" and *keqihua*, none of it considered part of the true content. Not only is it considered essential in relationship building, but it also serves as a "feeler" to get a sense of you and your intentions.

No. 3: Read Body Language
Reading body language will not only give you a clearer picture of what is really happening but also of who is making the decisions and how successfully the meeting is proceeding.

No. 4: Be There or Be Square
The Chinese prefer face-to-face meetings to any other form of communication. Do not use faxes, telephone calls, and emails as primary communication tools. You need to show up personally, and spend as much time as possible bonding with the Chinese counterparts.

No. 5: Find a Competent Local Translator
There are long-standing cultural differences between regions in China. To have a culturally unacceptable person from another region within China

translating for you can greatly affect your communication, and more importantly, your outcomes.

How about just saying "no?"

Helen always recalls a certain conversation with a senior French banking executive. He said: "Why do the Chinese never say 'no'? They always say, 'It is interesting,' 'Let us come back to you later,' or even 'Yes.'"

After hearing Helen explain at length why the Chinese would do so, he pondered for a long while and said:

"But we would much appreciate them simply saying "NO!"

Chapter 7
Chinese Relationships

Sharing the same bed but having different dreams
Chen Liang, Song Dynasty

An ancient Chinese fable tells of a mighty tiger who caught a fox to eat for his evening meal. However the cunning fox immediately protested saying, "How can you have me as your dinner tonight? You must know that I am ordained by the heavens to be the mighty king of all beasts in the forest. If you don't believe what I say, follow me and you'll see that without exception, every beast in the forest fears me."

To prove the truth of this statement, the mighty tiger agreed to the fox's proposal. The fox went ahead, and the tiger followed closely behind. All the wild beasts in the forest, all the hares, deer, and squirrels, ran away in terror upon seeing the approaching mighty tiger.

The tiger thought the beasts of the forest were truly afraid of the fox. He decided it would be wise not to eat the fox.

Like anywhere else, building relationships in a strange place with people who are "tigers" instead of "foxes" is critical. Trustworthy partners and loyal Chinese employees will set you apart. Equally important are the relationships and connections, 关系 *guanxi* you establish when you want to work with the Chinese.

There are key differences between the way the Chinese and the Western business people form and maintain relationships. The Chinese believe that the best decisions are made not only to ensure that the business interests of all parties involved are satisfied but also (and more importantly) to ensure that one's personal social status is maintained, or (better still) elevated, to gain more face, 面子 *mianzi* within the circles of influence and beyond. Mianzi is always an underlying factor.

Uniquely, the Chinese believe that business partners should be friends first. The first important step is to nurture a mutual friendship—face-to-face—preferably during informal occasions such as a Chinese banquet or by inviting the business partners to your headquarters for a site visit. The Chinese will never commit themselves to a serious business relationship without first getting to know who they are dealing with.

A Chinese Fox

A very successful Australian architecture firm started its first China project in 1993, and was immediately successful in winning projects and businesses as it rode on the great boom of real estate development across the nation. With the strong demand, they soon established offices in Shanghai and Beijing with local Chinese operators who had the appropriate credentials. Without much hesitation, the Chinese were appointed as managers and small shareholders of the rapidly developing China business.

For a long period of time, the firm had failed to obtain a business license in China, and relied solely on the local managers and "friends" in Shanghai, Beijing, and Guangzhou to use their ways and means to employ staff and operate the China business. This Australian tiger then realized that it had been associating with some Chinese foxes when the company set out to establish its first wholly foreign-owned enterprise (WFOE), ten years after the business started.

Things started to go terribly wrong. When they went to officially register their name in China, they discovered that the Beijing manager had established a competing practice of his own, with forty people, and registered the Australian company name (now very well-known) as his trademark in Beijing. The Shanghai manager had done the same—he registered their company name as a trademark a few years earlier in Shanghai, built his own practice with an office in the opposite building, and even got into a joint venture with the Guangzhou manager to register the trademark in Guangzhou! (Trademarks or business names can be registered nationwide or in each city/province for a smaller local fee.)

In addition to the company brand being hijacked by the Chinese managers, the Australian company was informed about other successful projects that they knew nothing about—clearly handled by the Chinese managers, including work on significant Olympics projects. The Australian government told them that they had been liasing with their so and so office, when, as far as they knew, no such office ever existed.

A bitter battle to wrest back their identity

The Australian firm filed its own national trademark with the Chinese bureau in September 2003. Five years later, their trademark registration was "still being processed." The Chinese owners of the trademarks in Beijing, Shanghai, and Guangzhou were doing everything they could (officially and unofficially) to stop the registration from going through.

Moreover, the two related Chinese firms in Beijing and Shanghai were suing the Australian firm for using their Chinese name! The previous Beijing manager built a substantial business on the back of all the work and reputation gained by the Australian firm. When Helen was at the Beijing airport in September 2007, she saw a large billboard advertising the Chinese firm. In this

> prime location, the firm claimed its status as a large international business with a long history and a few Australian operations. In 2007, the Australian firm sued the two Chinese firms in Shanghai. After three years of appeals, they finally reached an out-of-court settlement.

In this chapter, we examine how the Chinese view, form, and maintain various relationships, then focus on how Westerners can gain entry into these Chinese "circles" and form long-term successful relationships.

Business names and brands must always be protected as early as possible in any new venture in a foreign country. However, what we want to focus on are the issues related to people and some of the "Chinese lessons" that this Australian firm paid such a high price for. Clearly, the Chinese partners had very different agendas from those of the Australian business owners.

CHINESE "CIRCLES OF INFLUENCE"

The Chinese sense of connectedness means that they are conditioned to live not as individuals but as a connected part of networks. Most form and maintain their circles of influence, including family and business relationships, as the most important part of their lives. It is vital to understand how the Chinese form their circles of influence in life and how they view friendships and business connections differently.

As far as the Chinese are concerned, people outside such circles are regarded as strangers, and different principles apply when it comes to dealing with people who fall into the "stranger zone." The Chinese prefer to spend most of their time and energy within their circles of influence. The Chinese word for a "loner" is 离群 *liqun*—"leaving the group." If you want to form genuine long-term relationships with the Chinese, it is vital to enter their circles and then comply with their implicit rules.

In China, family and business relationships may have separate circles and many layers, which we call rings within the circle (see the model on the following page). People in the outer rings are usually less important as compared to the core family and receive lesser attention as compared to those in the inner rings. However, the law of 阴 *yin* and 阳 *yang* means that such positions are neither static nor permanent. Relationships can change and always will—depending on the circumstances.

Often circles are not isolated from each other. For example, people in the private-invested enterprises (PIEs) often mix business and family relationships. People from the state-owned enterprises (SOEs) and the public sector usually keep these two circles separate, although occasionally, one may find such circles merged.

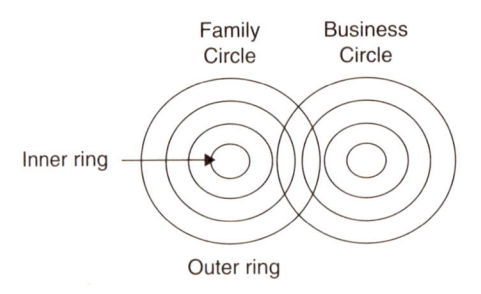

```
                Family      Business
                Circle       Circle
Inner ring ─────→

                Outer ring

          The circles of influence
```

The Chinese also have a very different sense of what comprises a family. Depending on the circumstances, this sense ranges from a nuclear family unit to a family that includes those born in the same region or town. These families form the basis of many important business relationships.

Family and relatives form the first circle of relationships—the private or personal circle. At the core are close family members—parents, children, spouse, and siblings. The outer ring comprises relatives—before the one-child policy of the late 1970s, most Chinese came from families with siblings and quite a few uncles and aunts. Also, for many people, those from the same village or township as the person's birthplace 老乡 laoxiang are regarded as being "related" and therefore fall within the family circle.

Usually, this circle remains stable apart from marriages, births, and deaths in the family. Occasionally, someone may move from the outer ring toward the center. For example, when a not-so-close relative is promoted to a very important role in the government or business sector, that person may be regarded as being closer to the center due to the relative importance of his or her position and elevated mianzi. Such promotions will bring changes to the way in which the relationship is maintained. The promoted relative may receive more visits or invitations to family gatherings, when previously he or she was not included. This is how the family acknowledges the promoted person's expanded mianzi.

The Five Layers of a Chinese Family

When the Chinese use the word "family," the sense is usually much broader as compared to the narrow Western definition of the nuclear family of parents and children, and sometimes, it is broader than other common definitions such as the traditional extended family in Italy and other European countries. At times, the term "family" may encompass members who are unrelated biologically or by marriage, but who have other connections, in the same way that in some cultures, people from the same region are called "cousins." The meaning of the word family can often change depending on the circumstances. The following are five layers that may apply when a Chinese talks about "family."

The nuclear three-generation Chinese family

This includes three generations: grandparents, parents, and children. Grandparents include in-laws from both spouses' sides.

This is the most common Chinese family unit. It is common practice for the family to get together at least weekly, usually at the grandparents' house for half or even a whole day. Some families also spend the entire weekend with relatives. In general, Chinese parents and children spend a great more time together than do Western families.

The Chinese have always been devoted to their family and children. It is regarded as the parent's duty to house, support, and look after the children until they get married. Some may live with their parents even after marriage, perhaps due to financial constraints. When married couples have children, the grandparents usually take care of the grandchildren until they reach schooling age.

The children are, in turn, expected to care for their parents and grandparents. For the past twenty-five years, families have been restricted by the one-child policy. This has resulted in parents focusing all their attention on just one child. While the policy has been slightly modified recently to allow two children in certain circumstances, it still exists and applies to most Chinese. In today's China, the majority are single-child families, creating a stark cultural difference from China's past.

Until recently, it was generally expected that children would provide for and look after both their parents and grandparents until they passed away. It was never expected that a social security system or nursing homes would replace that unwavering family support. However, a child now is expected to care for six aging relatives—parents, maternal grandparents, and paternal grandparents. The Chinese have a phrase, 上有老, 下有小 *shang you lao, xia you xiao*, that describes middle-age couples who not only have to look after their own young children but also their aging parents.

Those who fail to support their parents both financially and physically are criticized as 不孝 *bu xiao* (failing their duties of filial piety—one of the Confucian doctrine's six key elements). The word has meaning far beyond simply being irresponsible.

Ancestors

Traditionally, a Chinese family includes ancestors from previous generations (including those who have long passed away) and everyone with the same surname traceable through the family tree is connected.

The family, called 家族 *jiazu*, often has its own rules and regulations passed down through generations. The Chinese are very proud of their long family history, which dates back thousands of years. Some famous families can trace their ancestors and the details of their preceding generations. Probably the most famous is the Kong (Confucius) family.

Helen met a woman who was the twenty-third generation 代 *dai* of the Kong family—and was therefore related to Confucius. She proudly told Helen that she can see both her name and her five-year-old daughter's name in her long family tree.

People born in the same village, city, or region

The sense of a long family history and respect for ancestors also extends the sense of family to those born in the same village, city, or region. There is a Chinese saying that "one cries when one runs into a person from the same hometown" 老乡见老乡，两眼泪汪汪 *laoxiang jian laoxiang, liangyan lei wangwang*—acknowledging the underlying emotional link between two potential strangers.

Such an extended family sense is particularly strong when the Chinese move away from their birthplace, especially when they live overseas. For example, in most cities that have overseas Chinese communities, people from the same city or province form associations called 同乡会 *tongxiang hui*. The association often serves as a platform for a new migrant in the city to get oriented and form various relationships, including business connections.

Within certain ethnic groups, such sense of a family can be even stronger. When Helen worked with a Mongolian ethnic Chinese client to form overseas business ventures, he would meet with his fellow Mongolian friends in every European city that he would visit, after his business meetings. Their strong bond can only be described as that of an "extended family."

Close friends or business partners

A Chinese family can also comprise close friends or business partners. We shall look closely at the relationship between friends and business later. The concept of "friends are family" is reflected in the informal way in which the northern Chinese call their friends "brothers" 哥们 *gemen* or "sisters" 姐们 *jiemen*.

No one enters into a business relationship with a stranger. Many successful Chinese entrepreneurs will not conduct business with a stranger, no matter how good the deal is. They consider friends to be the core of their continued success.

Often, business partners spend more time with each other than with their real family members. Therefore, it is only logical for partners to become family members. Two of Helen's Chinese friends who are business partners became surrogate fathers to each other's children. When one is travelling, the other acts as the "father" of the partner's child. On one occasion, when the partner's child was ill, his friend drove both the child and mother to the local hospital in the middle of the night.

China as a country

The last concept of "family" for every Chinese is China as a country. Such a concept is not unique—anyone who is patriotic can relate to this. The strong emotional link between the Chinese and their nation is due to the cultural heritage and the long history that China has enjoyed. When the Chinese grow older, they are invariably drawn back to the motherland irrespective of where they have spent most of their lives.

There is a wonderful Chinese saying 落叶归根 *luoye guigen* or the leaves fall close to the tree, meaning that when the Chinese grow old, they spend the rest of their lives back in their hometown.

Circles of Influence in Business

When you are dealing with a prospective Chinese business partner, it is important to understand that the Chinese believe that business partners should be good friends too.

The Chinese "business or working circle" consists of friends, colleagues, business associates, and other connections, which may include school alumni associations, industry clubs, and so on.

At the core are the most commercially and strategically active relationships, including friends, business contacts, and government connections. The Chinese invest significant time and energy to nurture and grow such inner circles of influence. In fact, much of the eating, gift-giving, and many of the spa excursions are part of the effort to keep these relationships alive.

Case Study: *Global TechCo's Long March—Building Relationships the Chinese Way*

To welcome the founder of GlobalTechCo on his first visit to China, Carl had arranged a series of events offering the best possible "five-star" treatment. The founder was driven from the airport in a limousine, with a police motor arcade, after which he attended banquets with senior government officials. Next day, their photos were on the front page of the local newspaper.

Carl even introduced him to a celebrity girl friend, and they frequented top entertainment destinations where fine wine and company were plentiful. This must have gone to the head of a modest scientist who fell in love with China and his new friends, and with all he could do in this land of vast opportunities.

The outer ring of this circle also includes colleagues, alumni, and members of the same club or association.

Naturally, this circle changes with time, and people from the outer ring shift to the core, and vice versa. The ones who are successful are those who have mastered the fine art of balancing the relationships within their own circle, as well as positioning themselves strategically within the circles of others.

Different groups in the Chinese business community build different types of circles around themselves. People who work in the SOE environment will often have stronger links within the government, the Communist Party, and related agencies.

They often form networks within their own business arena and don't spend much time mingling with the other business sectors unless there is a particular reason. Also, their business and family circles work independently of each other, even when there are some interwoven parts. For example, it is very rare for a person from an SOE to attend business functions or go on a business trip with a spouse.

In the PIE environment, the circles are somewhat different. These Chinese entrepreneurs usually network with a mixed array of people. Most merge their business and family circles; their business relationships often overlap with personal ones as they operate family businesses. These Chinese entrepreneurs typically involve family members and relatives in their business ventures, as they are seen as being most trustworthy.

Case Study: *Global Techco's Long March*
Day 4—*Moving in Circles*

In the previous episode of negotiations after the fortuitous car accident, Tom received a verbal proposal to form a joint venture. He knew that the Board would not be interested in such a proposal, but still asked Mr. Wang to submit a written proposal so that he could present it to the Board. In the meantime, he asked Carl to arrange for another meeting with Mr. Hu, the key investor.

Tom was keen to explore the potential of the original proposal. He knew that his message had to reach Hu, so that a true picture of the company could be presented and the negotiations could move forward. Carl insisted that Hu was rather busy as he had been called to Beijing for an important government meeting, but Hu was doing his best to return to meet Tom.

After another meeting with Mr. Wang the following day, one that went around in circles, Tom got really frustrated and could not wait any longer. He went to visit Carl at his hotel and told him politely but firmly that he was leaving the next day, as he had already waited the whole week to see either Mr. Hu or the government leader but to no avail. If the Chinese were still interested in acquiring the company, they would have to come to Europe to visit him.

Why had Carl failed to arrange such an important meeting with Mr. Hu? It is said that in China, the degree of separation is not six. It is often only two or three. The quiet actual leader of this Chinese consortium, Mr. Hu, is one of the most successful entrepreneurs in the region. He put together a few successful listed companies and had built multiple strong government connections. When he was introduced to the deal, he saw the potential of the company's technology, and knew that he could put another company together using the technology as a critical centerpiece, while leveraging on local government support and the many available government grants.

Carl was first introduced to him via another entrepreneur through whom he had sourced his own goods for export. Capitalizing on Global TechCo as an opportunity, Carl moved into a closer circle of influence within Mr. Hu's network. However, despite this, he obviously could not control Mr. Hu and failed to convince him to meet Tom again. This was the real but unspoken truth.

Most Chinese in the PIE environment do not like dealing directly with strangers. Even if they engage other people to help run their business, key positions are still held by "real" family members and relatives. Government support is also regarded as being critical for business success; therefore, there are important government contacts in their networks.

The Chinese in the foreign-invested enterprise (FIE) environment have different circles. Typically, they place less emphasis on government relationships, but more on extensive networks with people who have similar backgrounds in their business sector. They are more accustomed to Western protocols and codes of conduct—both during and after business hours. Usually, they are happy to bring along their spouses or partners to the functions they are invited to. Many serve as best bridges into China as they are more familiar with both the cultures and the Western corporate protocols.

Chinese friends and strangers

The Chinese also have very clear views about friends and friendship. Friends are categorized into different types—friends to eat and drink with 酒肉朋友 *jiurou pengyou*, literally "drinking and (eating) meat friends"; ones to do business with 生意上的朋友 *shengyi shangde pengyou*; and ones to talk to and listen to 良师益友 *liangshi yiyou*, which translates into "teachers and good friends that you benefit from."

A Chinese teacher who is also a good friend of Helen explained to her that a successful Chinese business person should have many different friends.

There are friends who are great to play golf with and help with your game. They can teach you the perfect swing and take you to the best golf courses around town. But they are only good for playing golf with. There are friends who are best to eat out with. They always know where to go, what to order, and in the end, pay the bill. Again, they are only friends to have meals with. When one goes into business with these friends, it may and often does end in disasters.

There are also friends one does go into business with. They are trustworthy, business-savvy, and will make the venture a great success. But one does not necessarily play golf with them—they could be far too serious about winning and may get upset if you beat them. Consequently, you could lose the business partnership.

In other words, the Chinese are very careful about maintaining and utilizing their "business or working circle" friends. Most Chinese businesses exist because of such wonderful webs of guanxi.

The Chinese usually place people outside their family and business circles in the stranger zone. Some can even be mean or ruthless to strangers. They can often behave in an indifferent, rude manner. One only needs to enter a busy office lift, drive on a road in a Chinese city, or board a domestic flight in China to experience this attitude!

The Chinese usually feel comfortable only when they are operating within their own circles. The Chinese managers of the unfortunate Australian architecture firm discussed earlier must have put the Australians in the "stranger zone" and felt that they were not obliged to do the right thing by them. Without excusing the unacceptable behavior of the Chinese partners, the outcome may have been quite different had the Australians spent more time assessing the Chinese before embarking on such an important relationship. It would have been helpful if they had conducted appropriate due diligence checks to validate whether they were the right partners, and invested more in conducting business in China rather than leaving it all up to their Chinese partners.

The Chinese "frequent flyer program"

Next to their own mianzi, the Chinese regard guanxi as their most valuable asset—sometimes, guanxi can be passed down through generations within the family. If you want to build an important relationship or approach an important business partner, the most effective way is to find someone who knows that person to introduce him/her to you and later, return that person's favor with something of value. This acts like a "frequent flyer program" in which one accumulates points.

Once that person has made the introduction, you must ensure that his or her favor is, or will be, returned (points redeemed). It usually does not matter how quickly you return the favor, but it is important that the reciprocation is of a higher value than the help you were offered. Failing to do so may not only damage your relationship with the person who introduced you, but also you may no longer be welcome within his or her circles.

On many occasions, we have witnessed the unwitting actions of foreigners when they seek an introduction to a key person through a friend or business acquaintance in China. These foreigners often trample across the introducer (fail to issue any frequent flyer points) and exclude the person from any further dealings or communication. While the clumsiness of some foreigners can be excused in certain circumstances, such behavior is truly unacceptable to the Chinese and invariably leads to failure. The person you are introduced to will watch closely how you treat the introducer, and will be wary of and then pay little respect to you if the introducer is not treated properly. Not only will you be removed from the inner circles of the Chinese introducer's network, but also the person that you are introduced to will keep you at a safe distance, expelling you from the frequent flyer program.

Therefore it is essential to make sure that you understand the motives of the introducer (however subtle), and keep the person informed of your progress. Furthermore, suitable reciprocation must be ensured to sustain the relationship. The return favor does not have to be monetary, and the introducer might be perfectly happy to connect you with a contact to whom he or she owes a favor.

As mentioned above, this reciprocation must be of greater value than the favor received. Under all circumstances, you must acknowledge the kind deed. To use a banking analogy, when you make a withdrawal, you must compensate in the most appropriate way to keep the account balanced.

A Chinese friend of ours recently asked one of his media mates to help a young relative find an internship at the local TV station. His friend happily agreed to help, as it was a small favor. More importantly, this gave him the perfect opportunity to refresh his guanxi at the TV station. In the meantime, once he helped out our friend, the favor would be returned—in a larger proportion.

Remember that mianzi and guanxi are interwoven. China is very hierarchal and a person's position holds great value. Powerful alliances are built by sharing guanxi while ensuring that everyone has more mianzi along the way. To maintain and nurture vital and positive guanxi means that ultimately, the relationships will feed off each other and trusted circles of influence will be shared—while benefiting each other and elevating the mianzi of all concerned.

Obviously, forming such circles takes a long time, and the Western style of bonding will not work with the Chinese. When a Western function or an event is hosted in China, most Chinese will only attend to give mianzi to

> ### *A French Success*
> A prominent French financial institution established their first representative office in Beijing in the early 1980s. They invested a huge amount of resources in nurturing various relationships in China, particularly with the government at all levels. They even established an office in an inner Western Chinese city during the mid-1980s at the request of the local city government. Back then, there was hardly any foreign investment going into these Western cities; most foreign investment found its way to cities such as Beijing, Shanghai, Guangzhou, and a few others in the eastern coastal region.
>
> The CEO of the company told Helen that even though his decision was made mainly to support their Chinese friends—the city mayor and his team—it actually turned out to be very financially rewarding. The local government was truly pleased with their friendly gesture and in return, awarded them many projects to finance. Today, their organization remains the largest financial service provider in the city, funding most of the significant infrastructure projects.
>
> In this particular case, by attracting a large foreign institution into the city, the mayor made "politically savvy" move. Not only was his political career enhanced by this introduction, but he will also remember the French as "friends in need." Such favors are often returned, regardless of what form they take.

their foreign hosts. In the meantime, when a Chinese business owner hosts a get-together, only those deemed appropriate from inside his or her circle will be invited. Children's birthdays, wedding occasions, and other personal occasions can also be used for dual purposes, where both social and business relationship bonding can be achieved.

Can Foreigners Really Network With the Chinese?

One rule we always stick with is—never conduct business with a Chinese party that has never done business internationally. There is too high a probability that they will not understand your objectives and that the business relationship will fail.

Ask for recommendations and comments from people in the industry or the community and conduct due diligence and ensure that the potential partners are as enthusiastic as you about entering into a mutual relationship. If you have good intuition, trust it when identifying the Chinese as potential partners or employees.

Adopt a patient approach and be in China as much as possible to invest and build your own circle, including as many Chinese as possible. Do your best to accommodate a request from your local Chinese party even when it doesn't seem important to you. Remember, the gesture will be remembered and appreciated, as your Chinese partner will feel that their face is protected or elevated.

The "aliens"

Almost by definition, gaining entry into a Chinese business or social circle means socializing or networking with the Chinese. Unfortunately, we often witness expatriates gathering and socializing only among themselves. They go to the same functions, invite each other for parties and gatherings, and then complain about feeling alienated! (No wonder then that the name of the Chinese government bureau that looks after foreigners' affairs in China was once wrongly translated as "The Aliens Bureau!")

Remember, the Chinese often mix business with pleasure—but they work only with friends and/or their connections, or people that are referred by them. Should you have the opportunity to attend a Chinese gathering, try your best to accept the invitation. Even though the occasion may be very "Chinese," the invitation shows that the Chinese are making an effort to include you in their circles. By showing up not only will you give them mianzi, but also you will get an opportunity to observe and bond more with your potential partners by becoming friends.

However, do not try to connect to too many people, adopting a "scatter-gun" approach to your guanxi. It takes time and patience to develop focused relationships that will be rewarding in the long term. When you spread yourself too thinly in your attempts to make connections, it will have the opposite effect. Always remember that it takes time to build real relationships, and if you ignore or fail to maintain a relationship, it can be easily lost.

When Helen was working with her Mongolian Chinese client, she accompanied him and a group of European visitors to Inner Mongolia for a "business trip," which mainly involved sightseeing. The Mongolian Chinese businessman believed that the best bonding experience would be to show those future business partners his hometown and entertain them with countless banquets and traditional singing and dancing. The Europeans were exhausted after this Chinese-style bonding—however, they did appreciate the gesture!

"Heroes think alike"

How does one identify the right Chinese partner to work with? The saying "Heroes think alike" is a good principle for finding the right partner. Another Chinese saying "You should not consult or work with someone who doesn't believe in the same things that you believe in" 道不同不相与谋 *dao butong bu xiang weimou* is also applicable.

When your goal is to build a long-term, reputable, and professional business, it is vital that you find like-minded people, the Chinese "heroes."

You cannot succeed when your Chinese counterparts are those who pay lip service to your goal and have a completely different, but hidden agenda.

Some Chinese with short-term objectives think that as long as they can make money quickly, it does not matter how they make it. Some even believe that if they do not take advantage of others, then they themselves will be taken advantage of. They often think that there are unlimited numbers of people and businesses for them to manipulate, and the sheer size of China means that they can continue to act in such a way for a long time without being caught.

"Sharing the same bed but having different dreams"

This saying usually refers to couples in unhappy marriages who, for various reasons, still live together. In business contexts, this description describes business partners who enter into a mutual relationship with different objectives. If you want to succeed in China, it is vital to have the same objectives as your business partner.

Most of the unfortunate problems in foreign joint ventures have originated from partners having different goals. Sometimes, the fault lies with the foreign party failing to communicate effectively to the Chinese what they aim to achieve, putting the most important terms cleverly into legal documents without getting the points clearly across to the Chinese. At times, some things are left unsaid for strategic reasons. Some foreign businesses expect the contract that they sign with the Chinese to dictate the future business—they expect that all things agreed upon will be precisely executed as outlined, and that common understanding is ensured by such documentation. To the Chinese, however, the contract usually merely refers to rough guidelines for the future.

In other cases, the Chinese look to gain some financial, managerial, and overseas marketing advantage by knowingly entering into a relationship where their objectives are not completely aligned with those of the foreign party. The Chinese apply the law of yin and yang—things can change and always will—to the joint venture. To them, it does not matter that the objectives are not the same at the outset. Occasionally, this is because they don't fully comprehend the other party's objectives and feel that they will lose mianzi if they ask what may seem to be "naïve" or "simple" questions about legal documents or terms.

Also, they may assume that, as long as the main concerns that have been raised verbally by both the parties are satisfied, it is not worth paying attention to every written clause in a diligent manner.

For many Chinese, an agreement is often a formality—they don't want to bother with the fine details as they believe that those can be worked out later.

Short-term Thinking

Having spent a long time working overseas, Helen was often advised by her local friends that she was "too straightforward and trusting," with a largely Western mindset. Not paying enough attention to such warnings, she went into a 50/50 partnership with an old Chinese classmate who said that he would like to build a long-term professional business relationship with her. Within a year, this partner started carrying out side deals and told many stories to ensure that his own interests were protected and rewarded at the expense of the partnership, siphoning-off profits to his own separate companies.

Helen realized that he never trusted her in the first place, even though he claimed regularly that he did. He was making 忽悠 *hooyou* (a colloquial term originating from northern China which means misleading or exaggerated statements—bluntly, "bullshit"). He knew that Helen would take him at face value, being so used to the Western style of communication. While Helen was convinced that he was the right partner to build a long-term business relationship with, all he wanted was to ensure that he made as much money in the shortest time possible by conducting private deals on the side, outside the partnership.

One can see how such different expectations, when not handled very carefully, are most likely to take the partners on separate paths. It is quite common now for foreign investors to buy back the shares of their Chinese joint venture partners, or establish their own wholly owned entity to start all over again.

A small-minded person

The majority of the Chinese business community is ethical, professional, and focused on the long term. However, some do not have a long-term view, and tend to use dishonest or so-called strategic ways to maximize their wealth within the shortest time frame. This reminds us of a wonderful Chinese saying "A small-minded person will never understand how a person with integrity and vision thinks"—以小之心度君子之腹 *yi xiaoren zhixin duo junzi zhifu*. The saying can also be translated as "Don't gauge the heart of a 君子 *junzi* (an ideal, honest person with integrity) with your own mean measure."

We have both paid our dues while doing business in China. There were times when we entered into partnerships or joint ventures with friends, only to be taken for a ride.

In retrospect, with regard to the above case study, Helen is certain that while they were busy making money behind her back, they were convinced that she was doing the same. It is vital to avoid such small-minded, short-sighted people as they can only bring detriment to your business and reputation. A good French friend of Helen's once said that after years of working in China, his alarm bells always go off the moment he hears a potential Chinese partner start talking about long-term relationships and/or sincerity at their first meeting!

Are the Chinese Really so Different?

Understanding a person's background also helps in choosing the right person to deal with. There are a few ways to categorize the Chinese business people and here are a few tips.

No. 1: Understand Their Work History

Look at a potential contact according to the business strata they belong to—SOE, PIE, or FIE. Even though the Chinese may network mainly with people within their own group, we suggest that one should always meet and network with as many Chinese as possible—keeping in mind not to stretch oneself too thinly.

No. 2: Appreciate Their Background

The second way to categorize the Chinese is according to their age group, educational background, and work experience. Often, we find that people in their mid-30s to mid-50s with overseas education and/or work experience are the best "bridges" to work with when doing business in China.

No. 3: Where Do They Come from?

Another way of categorization is by regional groups. The Hong Kong Chinese are very different from the mainland Chinese, and the same is true between, say Taiwanese and Malay Chinese.

We often find that Western companies tend to think that the Hong Kong Chinese and the Taiwanese Chinese are "Chinese enough" to work in the mainland. The reality is that most mainlanders see Hong Kong and Taiwanese Chinese as "outsiders." When an international firm appoints an overseas Chinese to manage their mainland business, more often than not, there are cross-cultural issues between the Chinese; sometimes, even worse than those between the Chinese and the non-Chinese.

When a major international business acquired one of the leading online shopping portals a few years ago, they changed its top management and hired executives from Hong Kong. Soon afterward, most of the original shareholders and managers quit the business. The Hong Kong executives did not have the same in-depth understanding of mainland customers and the distribution relationships and the business suffered accordingly.

However, there are success stories too. Helen knows the Malay Chinese founder of a very successful London-based private equity firm investing in China. When she asked the founder about the secret of his success in China, his answer was, "hire good local people." In fact, not only does this firm hire local people, but also they have thirty-two offices in China—four of which are 100 percent owned and the remaining 60 percent owned with a local partner in regional China. A Hui Muslim Chinese partner heads their very successful Islamic Finance practice, serving the (estimated twenty million) Muslims in China. They have their own staff in the remote inner west regions (Xinjiang Province, for example), which enables them to secure and invest in business ventures that are almost impossible for other foreign private equity firms to access.

The Arrival of an Extra-Terrestrial (E.T.)

Finding a good local person is key to your business success. However, mainland China is as diverse as the United States or Europe, and must be treated regionally.

Some of the subtle regional cultural differences that the Chinese see among themselves are expressed in the following joke, which also highlights classic Chinese humor.

An unidentified flying object (UFO) discovered in China has an E.T. on board. Here are some expected reactions from the different regions:

- The people from Beijing will first discern the E.T.'s official ranking and which party he represents (very politically sensitive);
- The people from Shanghai will organize an exhibition straight away (to make money);
- The people from Henan will immediately make copies and export the E.T. copies to the rest of the world (localize and globalize!);
- The people from Wenzhou will send a business proposal to the E.T. to elicit joint venture opportunities (known for making business out of nothing—very entrepreneurial);
- The people from Guangzhou will clean the E.T. first, then work out the best way to eat it! (The Chinese have a saying, "To eat, one needs to go to Guangzhou"—as the people there are known for daring to eat anything).

Conclusion

So how do you know who to work with, how to connect, and when to walk away?

Our first suggestion is visit China as often as possible and stay for as long as possible. Remember that face-to-face communication is the preferred and most effective method. By meeting and bonding with potential partners, not only are you are forming your own Chinese business circle, but you are also given the opportunity to learn about China and your business partners or employees firsthand.

Next, find and build bridges. Work with the Chinese who have worked or lived overseas, especially those who have shown genuine interest and willingness to help. The many overseas-trained Chinese can conduct proper due diligence on your potential partners and managers. Never skip the normal care you would take in building business relationships in your own country and check the backgrounds and references of all those whom you deal with!

Chapter 8

Small Things

One leaf can block your view of the Tai Mountain
Anonymous

The Chinese are full of contradictions. Seemingly conflicting schools of thought co-exist harmoniously. It is natural for the Chinese to hold opposite, 阴 *yin and* 阳 *yang views simultaneously, then go with one instead of the other depending on the circumstances.*

For example, the Chinese saying above, "One leaf can block your view of the Tai Mountain," illustrates that too much attention to small or unimportant things can make one lose sight of the big picture.

However, the opposite saying is, "One could suffer greatly because of a failure to consider small things" 因小失大 *yinxiao shida. When one is unaware of the small things in China, those unfamiliar to a foreigner, one could be at a loss in understanding Chinese thinking.*

Many things annoy the Chinese when dealing with foreigners, and vice versa. This is not just etiquette, where the Chinese will accept the eating habits of a foreigner, seeing them as a result of their "unfortunate" upbringing. This chapter focuses on how things that seem small to foreigners can be sufficiently large in the eyes of the Chinese and can be interpreted in different ways to make life embarrassing. We use some very recent business cases to better prepare you for dealing with the intricate and complicated Chinese ways.

CAN FOREIGNERS BE "REAL" FRIENDS WITH THE LOCAL CHINESE?

Recently, Helen met an American couple who have been living and working in Beijing for more than five years. Both love China, its people and culture, and even their children (now studying in American universities) call China their home. They sincerely wish they had more "real" Chinese friends, but are frustrated that they have not made any so far.

They befriended a lovely local Chinese couple but were only recently invited over for the first time to the couple's house despite having had them over at their place many times.

Helen started pondering whether the non-Chinese could ever be true friends with the local Chinese, and why the Chinese couple would behave in this manner. The reasons could be many. However, one major issue could be "face" (面子 *mianzi*). The Chinese might feel embarrassed that their place is too small or not good enough to have foreign guests around. If inviting you to their home could make them lose mianzi, then no matter how frequently you invite them over, they will not reciprocate. And, more frustratingly, they will never tell you why.

The second major reason could be the choice of food and the environment. The Chinese often prefer eating out to having home-cooked meals and they would rather take you out to eat. A typical Chinese restaurant in China is usually very crowded and noisy. Most Westerners prefer a quieter atmosphere, but the Chinese don't mind such an environment at all. Also, there are more choices available on the menu, so they don't have to worry about having chosen the wrong home-cooked food for you.

Another reason is that some Chinese may still feel that a foreign friend is somewhat, well, "foreign." They find it difficult to see a person for who he or she really is, as the different color of the eyes, skin, and hair are barriers they have perhaps not yet overcome. Remember that modern China opened its doors to the world only over the last few decades. Most Chinese

---

He is Still a 老外 **Laowai** *(Foreigner)*

Helen graduated from Peking University, and most of her classmates from the same department remain good friends. They meet in Beijing few times a year. Having lived overseas for many years, Helen is used to gatherings where couples are invited and meet each other's friends. After she brought Geoff to a couple of events, she felt a sense of uneasiness in the air. Was it Geoff?

But when she first asked if she could bring her partner along, the answer was always "yes." Now she realizes that it was a "Chinese yes" which actually means "no!" So finally, when another reunion was scheduled, she asked again, "Is it really OK for me to bring my husband along?" One of her friends finally admitted that actually, he preferred not having Geoff around. To make sure that Helen was not losing face, he explained that it was only so that the conversation could be more relaxed and candid." He then added, "because after all, he is still a *laowai* (foreigner)!"

have very little intercultural experience. They are not accustomed to different physical appearances. Also, many may not be familiar with foreign cultures. Bear in mind that the unknown is usually what makes us scared or uncomfortable.

Also, the Chinese may not be very keen to have foreigners as friends possibly because they see that foreigners come and go. The transient nature of many foreigners in China hinders their acceptance into the Chinese community. Accepting a true friend is a long-term commitment, which means that you are in their inner circle of influence and connections—both for work and life.

In this particular case, maybe when the Chinese begin to realize that our American friends are here for the long run—and see that, in fact, they can be in many aspects more "Chinese" than a lot of other Chinese—perhaps many will open their arms and hearts to welcome them as true friends.

Overall, with the dramatic changes in China and the global village we live in today, there is no doubt that the younger generation of Chinese will definitely form real friendships with people from all around the world. As for the others, we hope it is only a matter of time before they realize that racial and cultural barriers are only skin deep.

Food is the Sky

Food is one of the most important things for the Chinese. While grabbing a quick bite to eat may not be important to the busy Western person, eating in China has significant cultural and business importance. The Chinese saying, "food is the sky" 民以食为天 *min yi shi wei tian*, indicates that food—and eating—are most important in sustaining life. One should always be aware of the Chinese "eating" phenomenon.

Chinese families spend huge amounts of money on birthdays, weddings, and funerals—mostly celebrating and socializing over banquets. For example, when a Chinese couple gets married, it is standard practice in the northern regions for the bride's parents to pay for newlyweds' furniture and for the groom's parents to pay for the wedding. On average, the cost of such a banquet will be equal to or more than the entire cost of furnishing their apartment.

Of course, the more the guests at the banquet table, the merrier it is. The more important or interesting the guests, the bigger the mianzi. When we first arrived in China as an exotic, interracial couple with a cute baby, we received many wedding invitations—even third-hand through friends of friends. Having a foreigner at your wedding gives even bigger mianzi, baby and all!

The Importance of Business Banquets

Food is not always as important as its social significance. For example, those who take leftovers (a doggy bag) from a restaurant meal will be generally regarded as "having no face"—even though the government is lobbying very hard to change that. An alarming statistic showed that in Shanghai alone, restaurants generate over 1,100 tons of leftovers every day!

Part of the reason for such waste, especially in the business context is that dining together is not at all about eating. Hosting a banquet for guests is the best way for the hosts to show their hospitality and respect toward their guests. The Chinese prefer to first establish an informal relationship with potential business partners. Eating together is a way to get to know each other in a casual setting that allows both parties to establish mutual trust and build 关系 *guanxi*. When two parties can sit down and do the most important thing together harmoniously—that is, eating food—then it is fine to trust each other in business!

Furthermore, eating is symbolic of showing good faith—"giving each other face" (给面子 *gei mianzi*), even though some Chinese themselves feel that such occasions are a waste of time and money. In fact, most Chinese business dinners start very early—usually at 6:00 p.m.—as they are considered to be part of the job. When one party pays for a meal, it is common practice for the other party to thank them by paying for the next meal—and so on. At each banquet, some expensive dishes must be ordered (for example, sea urchins, bird's nest, or shark fin soup) to show the host's respect for his guests. An elegant dining table inside a private dining room is often an extension of the boardroom table. Important business issues are often discussed and decided over a sumptuous meal.

There is a considerable amount of detail to learn about the interface between banquets and business dealings. Sometimes, even the Chinese get it wrong! For starters, we mention below some small but very important things to take note of.

Seating Order

Usually the seat at the middle of the table is reserved for the host (the most senior ranking person). His or her special chair position will have the napkin folded differently from the others. The most important guest sits on the right-hand side of the host; the next most senior-ranking guest sits on the left-hand side of the host, and so on. Everyone waits for the host to sit down before getting themselves seated.

Remember that China is very class conscious—if you are the host, do ensure that the seats for the Chinese guests have been prearranged according to their hierarchy or level of importance.

The Art of Toasting

When you are not the host, toast only if the host suggests it. The host usually proposes the first toast and after an appropriate time, guests should propose toasts in return.

Conversation at the Table

Do not raise any personal questions—related to the spouse or children for example—unless someone volunteers or asks you first. When the host stops discussing business and changes the topic, do not mention business again.

How and When It Ends

Wait until the host announces the end of a meal—it is regarded as rude for a guest to bring a banquet to an end!

New Age Banquets

On a busy business trip to Nanjing, the capital city of Jiangsu Province, Geoff experienced firsthand the "new age" banquet. He had a rushed trip and was busy meeting government officials on possible projects in the region. As they had to be at the airport by 8:30 p.m., an hour's worth of banquet was squeezed in at 6:00 p.m.

They were meeting a high-ranking official at the old British Ambassador's residence that had been converted into a restaurant for special meetings such as this one. They ate in a function room, previously the Ambassadors wife's bedroom. The room seemed to have been left as it was, with its lovely salmony-pink decor and the bed replaced with a dining table perhaps.

In precise movements, the officials arrived, having rushed from another meeting with a major American company also looking to invest in Nanjing. The banquet started immediately.

Geoff has attended numerous Chinese banquets, but this one was different. It was clearly truncated to suit the limited time, but these officials were efficient and focused on talking business immediately. Food was delivered to the table and toasts were made in record time with only one glass of red wine for each. No one wanted to get the other drunk with countless drinking games or toasts. Things proceeded with efficiency and timeliness. This new age banquet could become a thing of the future!

As most business-related meals are regarded as part of the job, these banquets usually start very early and last between one and two hours.

Who Should Pay

It is usually implied that the host will pay for the meal. However, the Chinese tradition is that one should at least offer to pay. You may notice that some Chinese even put up a physical "fight" over the bill. Usually, they are friends who want to show each other generosity and give each other mianzi.

A well-versed China hand would accept the generosity of the host after offering to pay in a sincere but not too aggressive manner, then thank the host profusely (it is a delicate balancing act that the Chinese have perfected into an art). Then he or she will also make sure the host knows that their hospitality will be returned.

Sharing the bill is not commonly acceptable in China—as it indicates that "we don't owe each other anything," which could further translate into "we are not connected!"

BIG THINGS FOR THE CHINESE: DO NOT BE SEEN IN A TAXI

In the case study "New Age Banquet" mentioned earlier, as Geoff's party left, the usual pleasantries were exchanged with the officials walking them to the front of the old residence. But then a small thing turned into a major surprise.

Geoff's party was with their local Chinese business partner—an energetic property developer, well known and obviously well connected, who had arranged for them to meet and greet all the right officials. Their party of four had arrived separately in two cars to the restaurant from different meetings. However, after dinner, Geoff's party had to make do with the Chinese partner's car—a lovely but small BMW 5 series waiting to take them to the airport.

As they stood around at the front of the old residence, Geoff saw the dilemma immediately—there were four of them, each with an overnight bag, and there was only one small car. Geoff opened the boot only to find that it was full of paper bags containing gifts. That was odd.

It was quickly shut by the perplexed-looking driver. Geoff realized that, as one of the major festive seasons was approaching, their local partner had stocked the car boot with presents to hand out to all her important contacts in Nanjing.

Geoff decided to hail a taxi as it was obvious that they were not going to fit into the BMW. He was quickly stopped and told quietly but firmly to get into the car. All this time, the government hosts were exchanging pleasantries with them, laughing and chatting, pretending not to notice anything unusual.

Then Geoff was literally shoved into the back of the BMW with his overnight bag, and the remaining three piled in with their bags. They drove off waving regally to the official throng on the steps. The car drove about 500 meters up the road before it stopped and they all fell out. The Nanjing contact apologized profusely, asked the driver to drop them off at the airport, hailed a cab herself, and then sped away.

On enquiring what was all that about, Geoff's Chinese colleagues looked quite serious and said, "We had only one car, and we could not call another cab on such an important occasion. So all of us had to get into the BMW to save mianzi."

Geoff asked, "But didn't it appear ridiculous that we were piled into the little BMW like sardines with bags packed to the roof on our laps?"

"Yes," they said, "but we left in style and saved face."

BIG THINGS FOR THE CHINESE: CHINESE FESTIVALS

The Chinese have always enjoyed festivals as an occasion for family gatherings and for taking some time off. Now days, more people have also started taking holidays. For the business community, however, festival periods are always regarded as the most important time for maintaining guanxi.

Before Helen's mother retired, half of her New Year holiday was spent calling on business contacts; the other half, visiting relatives. Now, she mainly keeps in active contact with the numerous relatives (some blood-related, some from her hometown).

During major Chinese festivals—Chinese New Year, for example—a week of official holidays is typically spent visiting relatives, dining together at one invitation, then another. There are also guanxi visits and banquets that not only honor the tradition but also present a perfect opportunity to give presents, refresh relationships, and, sometimes, to work on the next business opportunity.

Millions of migrant workers—both white collar and blue—return to their hometown to be with their families. For many, this is their only break for the whole year. Over 700 million people traveled by train during the 2011 Chinese New Year.

However, these traditions are slowly changing due to Western influence. Some of the younger generation choose to go away during the "intense banqueting" periods—to enjoy themselves or to limit their activities to a much smaller group of close relatives. Also, thanks to mobile phones (approximately a third of the Chinese population have mobile phones), text messaging has become the main tool for keeping in touch with friends and business connections. For example, in 2006, on the mid-Autumn Festival day (the fifteenth day of the Chinese Lunar August), the Chinese sent two billion text messages to each other!

BIG THINGS FOR THE CHINESE: APPROPRIATE GIFTS

The importance of gift-giving can never be overlooked, especially during the holiday seasons. Giving gifts can be extremely important and effective when doing business in China. In particular, if you come from a foreign country, bringing something small but relevant to give to your hosts will be much appreciated and helps to start a relationship on a note of sharing. Going the extra mile to identify your hosts' interests and giving them something personal really makes a huge difference. It is important to remember that, for the Chinese, first impressions count.

Usually, there are corporate policies regarding gifts in most companies. Often the gifts will be displayed on the corporate mantelpiece or used in the office. When the gift is personal in nature, the receiver may keep it for himself or herself.

This may not come as a surprise, but the Chinese do have different taste in gifts. In general, we find that anything that improves one's health (or damages it—cigarettes for those who smoke) and any quality food goes down well with the Chinese. French wine, Belgian chocolates, and Australian fish oil tablets will be warmly welcomed by your hosts.

"Hairy Crabs"

Remember our good friend from Nanjing and her BMW boot that was full of gifts?

There is a lake near Nanjing that is famous for its hairy crabs—small hairy lakeside crabs, sweet and much sought after. It was the best time of the year for eating these crabs and our friend was keen to deliver them to her network of colleagues and contacts in Beijing, just before the festival.

With her car packed with hairy crabs and RMB 1 million (US$120,000) in cash, they sped toward Beijing—a good 20-hour drive via the expressway. On the way, the driver had a major accident and was rushed to hospital. In the chaos, the crabs spilled everywhere and disappeared (along with the cash).

Leaving aside what happened and who was to blame, our friend had to first quickly engineer damage control. She faced potential worse harm if she did not deliver the hairy crabs to Beijing as she'd promised them to many important people. To disappoint them could mean a great loss of face and could ruin the relationships she hoped to strengthen!

Geoff's colleague in Beijing was enlisted and asked to go to the airport a few nights later to rendezvous with a night flight from Nanjing that not only had the hairy crabs on board but also the crab farmer, who was to accompany the crabs from the farm to the delivery point at Beijing airport. To lose your hairy crabs once is forgivable—but not twice! The airport was crowded and all flights were full, so the hairy-crab farmer (who had never been on a plane before) was given a first class ticket to fly with his crabs!

Geoff's colleague had gone to the airport to collect a VIP who was keen to be an early recipient of the sweetest crabs. The plane landed after midnight; there was construction underway on the way to the airport, and a traffic jam. It took two hours to get to the airport, find the cargo area, and eventually locate the crabs. All this while, the farmer waited, sitting on top of his hairy crab boxes with instructions to deliver it to one person only—Geoff's colleague.

As dawn broke over the airport, they finally sorted the crabs and loaded them for the trip back into Beijing. The VIP had his hand-picked hairy crabs (the cream of the crop) and he went off happily.

All ended well and much face was saved. Our friend was greatly relieved and pleased with all our efforts. Helping her "save face" was important for us—even if we only got a few hairy crabs for the effort!

WHEN BIG IS SMALL: WHEN CHINESE MR. NEAR ENOUGH MEETS THE DETAIL DEVIL

The Chinese are mostly big picture thinkers, meaning they are not big on details. This is part of the Chinese holistic thinking phenomenon. The West has a lot to offer the Chinese with regard to attention to detail. In observing the way the Chinese conduct themselves, a foreigner could be excused for thinking that the Chinese believe that "near enough is good enough." An American friend who has spent most of the past thirty years in China says that he has met countless Chinese Mr. Near Enoughs 差不多先生 *chabuduo xiansheng*.

A common view in China is that if something looks good from a distance, then it must be good. We have met many frustrated foreign builders who complain about the lack of finish work in a building. While Chinese builders can do marvellous things with concrete and steel, they have no real eye for detail when it comes to the final finish. If it looks good and works, "Why bother?" seems to be their attitude.

A possible reason for this could be the haste to secure a market or to make money. In the rush to catch up with the West and to leapfrog over old systems and processes, corners are cut and details are overlooked. In Chinese cities and streets, rubbish is piled high in very prominent areas, sometimes with no regard for public hygiene.

This type of Chinese thinking is best captured by the saying, "I clean the snow only in front of my own house" 个人自扫门前雪 *geren zisao menqian xue*. The outside area is of no concern to those who live inside the house or apartment. So even when the area right in front of a Chinese family's door is piled with rubbish, they turn a blind eye and walk past it, thinking that it is not their responsibility!

The "near enough is good enough" mentality contrasts sharply with the Western belief that "the devil is in the detail." We mentioned earlier that the Chinese dislike reading a legal document, particularly when they believe that the terms may change later. Often, they will sign the document without fully comprehending the legal or the commercial obligations, considering them to be "small things" that can be dealt with later if issues arise.

To the Chinese, a contract is regarded as the starting point of a relationship, providing some basic ground rules and a framework to protect all parties in the broad sense. However, given that things always change—particularly in China—they would rarely refer to the contract as the rules by which to proceed. There is a general sense that once things are written down, they are in the past and no longer of much relevance for the future!

The best strategy is to recognize that a signed contract alone is not enough. Constant communication and proper monitoring and control systems are required to make sure the Chinese counterparties appreciate that what they signed off is very important to you and that executing the agreement to their best ability will ensure a mutually rewarding and sustainable relationship.

First Impressions Do Count

The Chinese will generally make a quick decision about who you are based on first impressions. It is therefore very important to be prepared and to present yourself well. When the Chinese meet other Chinese, they invariably ask three questions to make an immediate assessment of each other, one that has a lasting effect on their opinion of one another:

1. What province do you come from (where is your father's ancestral home)?
2. What town were you born in (where is your family located)?
3. Which university did you graduate from?

A degree of formality always exists in business meetings. To show up in a pair of jeans and sneakers will leave a lasting, negative impression. Often, busy Chinese decision makers will give you only one chance to present yourself and your business. Understand how important this one meeting can be (regardless of the venue—we have had meetings in Mongolian huts, tea houses, and hotel coffee lounges). Be prepared to ask for what you want and take advantage of the opportunity to leave the best impression possible. It is best to be a little circumspect when you first meet a potential partner in China. Remain vigilant, let your host do the talking, and allow them to take the initiative.

Say little until you are ready to and have sized up the circumstances and your potential partners. Silence is never regarded as a weakness in China. On the contrary, you will be regarded as being wise and respectful—at least until you begin to speak.

WHEN SMALL IS BIG

Often in China, what sets one business apart from the others is attention to detail and getting the small things right. Helen attended a "disastrous" meeting, which demonstrated that when some seemingly small Chinese nuances are not cared for, the damage caused can be beyond repair.

Be Prepared—Meeting Protocols

To support a business partner based in Europe, Helen accompanied his client, a Canadian lady, on a visit to a Chinese government department that administrated the dairy industry. The Canadian lady works with a few diary producers to expand their market reach in Asia. The head of the Chinese party who met them along with her team was an intelligent, smartly dressed lady in her mid-fifties.

Unfortunately, it occurred to Helen very quickly during the meeting (and a little too late) that her European colleague had not briefed his client about

(Continued)

(*Continued*)

Chinese meeting protocols. She made a number of critical errors in this very Chinese meeting.

The Canadian client kept jumping in too quickly when the Chinese leader across the table was pausing for her translator to speak. It serves no purpose to interrupt when your host is beginning the meeting and needs time to raise all the major issues.

She made pointed comments implying that China needed a lot of help, particularly in the dairy industry. Any such comments, no matter how well intentioned, need to be delivered very tactfully. The Chinese are proud, patriotic people who value their mianzi more than anything. Helen noticed the subtle change on the face of our Chinese hostess—the bright smile had vanished completely, and she sat up with her arms folded, leaning forward.

This client, completely oblivious to the raised hackles, then started to address her questions to the other Chinese members. This is totally understandable as in the West, people are encouraged to engage everyone present at a meeting. However, in China, doing this implies disrespect to the most senior person present. Our hostess told the translator not to translate for the other Chinese members in the team; she told her team bluntly that they were not required to answer the questions.

By now, Helen could sense that the meeting was going to end abruptly. The Chinese hostess started to pack all our cards away and began complimenting Helen's client on her clothes. Helen was disappointed that the client had lost a valuable opportunity to establish some powerful connections, but the client walked away from the meeting blissfully encouraged by the friendly comments—especially about her dress!

Small things can turn big in China. Much revolves around language and communication. Many Chinese speak English, which can be a comfort, but beware as it may not seem as it appears. Confusion can turn on a small misunderstanding and deals can be lost.

Case Study: *Global TechCo Long March: Confusion*

Carl, our confused intermediary in the Global TechCo saga, had made a critical error by running off at a tangent embracing the founder. When Helen caught up with him in Kunshan, she had to spend most of the afternoon explaining repeatedly in very clear Chinese that the actual decision maker was Tom and not the founder and that Tom could either recommend the deal to the Board, or terminate it during his time in China.

Carl was genuinely shocked on hearing this.

The Chinese may find it embarrassing to admit that they don't understand your English. It is absolutely essential to repeat, speak slowly, or use translators when expressing critical messages. Even when the Chinese person is conversing in good English, one should never assume that they understand all. In particular, when specific vocabulary (terms related to technology or finance) is used, it is vital to ensure that a competent interpreter is available—one that you have chosen, not the one provided by the Chinese counterpart.

SMALL THINGS THAT ANNOY CHINESE

There are a few more unspoken things that generally unsettle or annoy the Chinese—especially those who are not accustomed to dealing with foreigners.

- Don't throw your business cards or money at people—this is regarded as rude behavior. Business cards are best presented with both hands and not slid or thrown across a meeting table. Some foreigners hand out cards as though they are dealing at a poker game. It makes us cringe and we know it unsettles the Chinese.
- After you receive a Chinese name card, always make sure you spend enough time reading and studying it before putting it away; this shows that you respect the person who just presented you with the card.
- Make sure you address the person correctly. Chinese surnames are usually spelled in front of their names (e.g., CHEN Hairong). Usually, they prefer to be addressed by their surname (e.g., CHEN, Mr. Chen) rather than their first names. Also make sure that you understand their titles—but never ask them to clarify their position in public during meetings.
- When you sit at the meeting table after exchanging the name cards, it is acceptable to lay them out in front of you, and it certainly helps to know the name of the person sitting across from you. However, if you do this, never put the cards away during the meeting as it will signal that the meeting has come to an end—at least from your side.
- Inappropriate comments or questions about China or its politics will most likely insult your Chinese hosts—especially comments about Tibet, Taiwan, or religious groups. Such topics are often taboo. As we saw earlier with our Global TechCo case, even singing Taiwanese karaoke songs can be politically offensive.

> **Case Study:** *Global TechCo Long March: A Small Thing*
>
> When Carl first called Helen, he told her that he was not going to pick Tom up from the Shanghai airport and that he would leave it to Helen to look after Tom.
> This came as a surprise to Helen as most Chinese will personally go to the airport to meet their distinguished foreign guest, irrespective of who is travelling as their companion. Tom was the CEO of the company Carl was seeking to work with and make an impression on. To show respect and face, one would most certainly expect Carl to pick Tom up from the airport.
> Helen's immediate interpretation was that Carl thought he was in a commanding position supported by his thinking that the founder was the real decision maker—not Tom, even though Tom's title was CEO.
> In China, many founders of enterprises retain the power to make important decisions—Carl had assumed that was the case here.

- Yelling or raising your voice at meetings or in public is a major irritant to the Chinese and is definitely unacceptable. However, if you are drunk with your hosts and singing karaoke, all will be forgiven and laughed off.
- As an inward-looking nation, the Chinese are not very physical. They refrain from touching, let alone kissing (even socially). Shaking hands is acceptable, but hugging and kissing can be very embarrassing for men and especially for women.
- It is important to never abuse a person's network or group when entering the inner circles of a close network. To abuse a Chinese introduction by not paying sufficient respect to the introducer (financially or otherwise) can lead to a very short-lived career or business in China.

SMALL THINGS THAT ANNOY FOREIGNERS

A number of small things are potentially annoying to a foreigner. Do your best to appreciate these differences and be open minded. By not judging others through our own lenses, these things can be easily explained and tolerated. These include the following:

- The Chinese don't always look a person in the eye. Don't be confused or annoyed by this. To the Chinese, looking someone straight in the eye can be regarded as disrespectful.

> **Case Study:** *Global TechCo Long March: A Private Cigar Bar*
>
> The key person behind intermediary Carl was Mr. Hu. When he met Tom during an earlier visit, he had insisted on showing Tom the cigar bar behind his office. His company occupied the entire eighteenth floor of an office tower. Half of this space was his office, complete with a bedroom, a ping-pong table, a game room, and a library.
>
> An electronic door behind the office led to a cigar bar–meeting room; reputedly, the most exclusive "business club" one could get into.

- The Chinese don't always give way to a female (although "women carry half the sky," as Mao once said). When entering into a lift, a room, or a car, it is more appropriate to "give face" to the most important person. Generally, the most important guest enters a door or a lift first.
- The Chinese may ask questions such as, "How old are you?" "How much is your house worth?" "What is your religion?"—as they have a different set of criteria for sensitive and private questions.
- While the Chinese are wonderful hosts, Westerners may suffer "hospitality overload." They may arrange your itinerary to the minute, filling every day with sightseeing, shopping, and banquets—in addition to business meetings. They may also swamp you with helpers and guides, when you just want to be left alone. Proper management is the key, but don't inadvertently offend your hosts—they are simply trying to give you mianzi, and hoping to make you feel comfortable in the best way that they know.

While you are not expected to embrace all Chinese customs, it is good to know what to expect and not to be caught by surprise.

ANSWER THAT PHONE!

One last comment on Chinese thinking and priority setting relates to the perpetual behavior of most Chinese with their favorite business device—the mobile phone.

We have no particular theory on why the Chinese believe that mobile phones are the most important extension to their bodies, and that the phone must always be answered when it rings. Phones are answered in the toilet, in the bath, in crowded restaurants, at critical moments during speeches at conferences, and, more annoying than anything else, during extremely important business meetings that you may have arranged! While in the West, most people prioritize the use of a mobile phone and apply discretion, the Chinese attend to any number of phone calls as they manage their operations and decision making on a minute-by-minute basis.

So while you fume at your next meeting about the frequent use of mobile phones even during your important presentation, remember, it is not personal. As time is extremely critical for all things "business," the mobile phone generally transcends most, if not all, interactions.

Do not despair. Know, too, that when you meet a really important person in China, you will undoubtedly have their undivided attention. In most cases, Chinese VIPs do not carry their own mobile phones.

CONCLUSION

So how do you develop and adapt a balanced approach for China? Remember that "small things" can make a big difference—sometimes, it pays to compromise or give to your Chinese counterpart something seemingly small, in return for what is important for you. In such situations, the Chinese will feel that they are given mianzi, and it is most likely that they will return the favor. It is helpful to work out the "wish list" for both yourself and your Chinese counterpart.

True partnerships or great deals happen only when both sides complement each other in a harmonious way. Be crystal clear about your priorities and be prepared to compromise on some less important issues to ensure that your top objectives are met. When you can balance your own wants and needs with those of the Chinese, you are not far from achieving the results you desire.

When it comes to balancing big and small, adapting the Chinese midstream approach may provide a key. Helen recently met with the Chinese managing partner of a very successful American fund investing in pre-initial public offering (IPO) Chinese state-owned enterprises (SOEs). You may know that many overseas companies refuse to invest in SOEs due to the difficulty and time it takes to reach an agreement, and because of the very different ways in which the SOEs approach business as compared to the West.

This fund, however, has been able to generate returns of 150 to 200 percent (on average) per annum. Because of its impressive track record, they have been able to attract more rounds of investment from the United States. When Helen asked the young executive about the firm's secret in investing in SOEs, he said wisely, "It is all about achieving a balance between controlling and letting go."

Working, living, and doing business in China is a constant balancing act. There is no exception when it comes to the conundrum of not losing sight of your larger China vision while still being aware of the seemingly small or insignificant things—from local customs to Chinese etiquette, business principles, and unspoken rules. Achieving this fine balance will open up a whole new world.

Chapter 9
Dealing with Conflict

Make the big things small and the small things go away
Anonymous

Many centuries ago in the shadows of a mountain, a shrine was built to honor a faithful tiger that stood by an old woman who had been seeking justice in a harsh world.

The story goes that this old woman had only one son. One day he went up into the mountains and was eaten by a tiger. The lady was so overwhelmed that she did not wish to live anymore.

Overcome with grief, she ran down the mountain seeking retribution and told her story to a local magistrate who laughed and asked her how she thought the law could deal with this tiger? But the old woman wanted to see justice done and refused to leave. In time, the magistrate lost his temper and threw her out of court. However, the lady was persistent and continued to implore the magistrate. Showing some compassion, he promised to have the tiger arrested.

She did not go home until the warrant for its arrest had been issued. The magistrate, at a loss of what to do, asked his attendants which one of them would undertake the task. Only one, Li Neng, who happened to be gloriously drunk, stepped forward and said that he would execute the warrant. The warrant was immediately issued and the old woman went away pleased that at last, justice had been done.

On sobering up, Li thought that the whole episode was a mere trick of the magistrates to get rid of the old woman, so he did not bother executing the arrest warrant. "Not so," cried the magistrate, "you said you could do this, and now I shall not let you off."

Li, at his wits' end, begged to enlist the best hunters to help him. Gathering a team, he spent days and nights in the mountains in the hope of catching a tiger (any tiger!) to at least show that he was fulfilling his duty.

A fruitless month passed. His failure in capturing the tiger led to a repeated punishment of several hundred blows with a bamboo cane. In despair, he went to a mountain temple and prayed and wept for forgiveness.

In time, a tiger walked into the temple, and Li froze, thinking he was going to be eaten alive. But the tiger took no notice of him and remained seated at the doorway. Li then addressed the animal: "O tiger, if thou did slay that old woman's son, humor me and let me bind you with this cord." Drawing a rope from his pocket, he threw it over the animal's neck. The tiger drooped its ears, allowed himself to be bound, and followed Li to the magistrate's court.

The tiger was put on trial and the magistrate asked, "Did you eat the old woman's son?" To this, the tiger replied by nodding his head, whereupon the magistrate stated: "Murderers should suffer death under the law. Besides, this old woman had but one son, and by killing him you took from her, her sole support in her declining years. But if now you will be that son to her, your crime shall be pardoned."

Again, the tiger nodded in agreement, and the magistrate gave orders for his release accordingly. The old woman was highly incensed, thinking that the tiger ought to have paid with its life for the death of her son.

Next morning, however, when she opened the door to her cottage, there was a dead deer lying at her doorstep. By selling its meat and skin, the old woman was able to purchase food. The tiger continued to do so frequently and sometimes it would even bring her money and valuables, so that she became quite rich, and was much better cared for than even by her own son.

Consequently, she became very well-disposed to the tiger, who often slept on the veranda, remaining there for a whole day at a time, giving no cause for fear to man or beast. Years passed, the old woman died, and the tiger roared with great sadness.

With all the money she had saved, the old woman was able to have a splendid funeral. While her relatives were standing around the grave, the tiger rushed out. While they fled in panic, it went up to the mound, roared like thunder, then turned and disappeared. A shrine was built on that very place in honor of the faithful tiger and it remains standing to this day.

The law operates differently in China and the West. The Chinese have a fundamentally different attitude toward dispute resolution. Where Westerners share a heightened sense of protection from their legal system, most Chinese have an aversion to confrontation and seek to solve problems in their own "Chinese" ways rather than seeking justice through the legal system.

Most foreigners recognize the evolving nature of today's young Chinese legal system and have well-placed fears of its ability to protect their investments and solve disputes. However, China has great potential of not only becoming a key compliant member of the world's legal society but also sharing its more compassionate approach to dispute resolution.

Throughout this chapter, we look at the Chinese legal framework and present a snapshot of its current legal system. The legal sector is going through a tremendous change. We also examine the Chinese attitude toward conflict and dispute resolution, as well as their approach toward this in both life and in business. We also explain how such an approach came about, and leave you with some suggestions to get the best out of a potentially difficult situation.

Historical Context

To gain a comprehensive understanding of the legal landscape in China, it is essential to examine the historic context first. In the following section, we explain where the legal system came from and the influence of Legalism, an important political philosophy.

The Ruler Makes the Rules

It is important to remember that for thousands of years, China was ruled by individuals (emperors, warlords, or dictators—sometimes all three), and not by legal systems. Although China has records of established judicial systems dating back as early as 4,000 years ago from the Xia Dynasty, such systems were primarily used as tools to safeguard social order and organize the people. In general, whoever had power created the rules, and their primary objective was to enforce and enhance the emperor's reign over a harmonious agricultural society. The legal system was a supplement to the ruler, not a tool for the governed.

Influence of Legalism

Legalism, one of China's most important political philosophies, emphasizes the need for order and social organization, and is based on the fundamental belief that "men are born evil." It assumes that everyone acts according to one principle: Avoid punishment while simultaneously attempting to achieve gains. Therefore, laws must be established, and rulers and authority must be respected. Legalism provides a framework for social and political order. It is not, however, a body of jurisprudence that outlines laws in the same way as the Western systems.

The two most famous Legalists were both students of Xun Zi (c. 313–238 BC), a well-known and influential Confucianist during his time. Legalism reached its height during the Qin Dynasty (221–206 BC) when one of the students, Li Si, a famous legalist and chancellor of the fuedal state and later of the Qin Dynasty, helped Qin Shihuang (始皇 *shihuang* refers to the first emperor) unify China using Legalism as the guiding principle. During his rule, all other schools of thought were outlawed. Li then served as prime minister for both Qin Shihuang and the succeeding emperor. He masterminded and implemented sweeping political reforms based on Legalist teaching, which formed the foundation of the government structure. These political structures and systems were used as the basis for many dynasties that followed.

Han Feizi (born c. 280 BC), prince of the royal family during the Warring States Period and the second famous student of Xun Zi, successfully combined previous Legalist thought and put forth the theory that a ruler can control a country on the basis of three concepts: Power can be maintained by analyzing the trends and gathering essential information; certain techniques or "secrets" can make it difficult to determine what the ruler is thinking so people will be motivated to follow the laws instead of "second-guessing" his thoughts (术 *shu*); and laws (法 *fa*)—a carefully devised code of rules, coupled with an administrative body would stringently and impartially police these rules and severely punish even the most minor infractions.

During the Han Dynasty (c. 130 BC), Emperor Han Wudi reinstated Confucianism as the only official teaching (which firmly established the dominance of Confucianism in China). However, Legalism as a political theory continued to heavily influence every dynasty.

Cultural Context

Chinese culture also manifests in how people perceive conflicts, litigations, as well as the action taken subsequently. Again, we can trace back such attitudes and behavioral patterns to Confucian teachings.

The Ideal of "No Litigation"— A 2,000-Year-Old Dream

For over 2,000 years, most of the benevolent emperors endorsed the teachings of Confucius to support their reigns. The teachings promote an ideal social order of five basic relationships and rank them in the order of subordination. These relationships lead to moral rules and a focus on self-discipline. Each relationship dictates that the individual is responsible for his or her role in life.

According to Confucius, the benevolent emperor, 仁君 *renjun*, should rule with love and care. "When people are led by laws and uniformity among them is sought by punishment, they will do their best to escape punishment and will have no sense of shame. When they are led by virtue, and uniformity is sought among them through the practice of ritual propriety, they will possess a sense of shame and come to you of their own accord."

One of Confucius' teachings was the ideal of a "no litigation" society (无讼 *wusong*). His idea became the fundamental thinking behind China's traditional legal system. The rule for the Chinese is: "Do unto others as you would have them do to you." Ideally, every Chinese should do his or her best to live harmoniously among others without hurting or damaging them. This is also closely linked to the concept of 面子 *mianzi* (face). Seeking justice via the legal system is regarded as shameful and immoral

> ### Case Study: *Global TechCo Long March: Conflict*
>
> In the unravelling set of circumstances in Kunshan had taken place in the West, everyone could have retreated behind the barricades and called for their lawyers.
>
> What did Helen choose to do when all was falling apart? Carl had manufactured a convenient car accident late at night, possibly buying time while clearly looking for solutions. Helen chose a non-confrontational path, leaving room for Carl to save face and retreat.
>
> Notwithstanding all her reservations about the ethical nature in which Carl was operating, she visited him at his hotel room, with witnesses, and included him in the discussion in the full knowledge that he was manipulating the circumstances, seeking a solution to his dilemmas.
>
> Tom and Helen tactically retreated to Shanghai, a larger city where they felt more on common ground with Carl and his cronies. At that point, it was clear that this trip (and probably the deal) was coming to an end.

conduct—where you have the potential of losing face or making your opponent lose significant *mianzi*.

An ideal person or an admired family takes pride in having no litigation in their family history. Therefore, most disputes are mediated or resolved in friendly ways. Usually, the most respected member of the family, village, or region will be asked to chair such important negotiations.

Most Chinese still have the mindset of "turning to the law only as the last resort." Problems are mostly sorted out among parties without any court involvement. Lawyers (trained or otherwise) are mostly hired as consultants to mediate the situation. Even today, most issues, including business disputes, are dealt with in informal ways.

Reality: The Modern Legal System

As litigation was regarded as a disgraceful action, and parties involved were looked down upon, a heavily structured legal system was not neccessary. Family-law-related disputes were mostly solved according to tradition, or "family rules" (家规 *jiagui*) that had been passed down within a family. The most respected person in the family (usually the most senior male) or the village, acted as the mediator.

Although most emperors promoted the ideal of a no litigation society, a legal administration system did exist to enforce the ruling.

Traditionally, all government offices also served as local courts. Government officials were judges and mediators. When the parties in a dispute failed to reach a resolution, they went to these local officials for another round of mediation.

The primary task of the local government officials was to mediate and assist people to solve the dispute among themselves rather than to prosecute anyone. When that failed, they would act as judges and conduct a hearing at the local government office. Offenders acted as their own lawyers, and the prosecution was not generally challenged in the legal sense. In addition to promoting a high moral standard for society, various means were developed to mediate, postpone, and resolve litigation in its early stages. However, such an "ideal" had its downside, as many sought to avoid interference with their daily activities. Further, the Legalist school of thought applied "reward and punishment" as its means of enforcement.

Some Chinese do not believe that the system can solve their problems and are disillusioned with the traditional system.

One cause of this disillusionment is the belief that there is always "room for interpretation." Traditionally, judges have a special power called "compassionate sentences" (恤刑 *xuxing*) and can interpret the law according to their own judgment, based on the situation before them. For the elderly, disabled, or junior offenders, a lighter sentence is regarded as reasonable. Unfortunately, this also leaves substantial room for unfair hearings and the possibility of wrongful rulings.

Another cause of disillusionment is that the court is regarded as a place for the rich and influential only. This is reflected in the well-known saying, "When you have justice, but not money, you should not be thinking of going to court."

In the past, a very small percentage of the Chinese resorted to "alternative" methods to right perceived wrongs—by using illegal means, hiring gangsters, or taking the law into their own hands.

Even today, while a majority of the Chinese adopt a do nothing or put up with it approach, such alternatives are still being used.

In China, only a very small proportion of disputes go through the legal system. There are ways to handle these disputes well; conversely, insensitivity to Chinese attitudes can lead to complete disasters.

While it is comforting to witness the progress the Chinese legal system is making, things may still go wrong. A person cannot simply seek to apply their Western concepts of justice to the Chinese legal system.

Background of the Modern Legal System

The introduction and adoption of "the rule of law" from the West did not start until the 1840s, when parts of China were colonized. A nascent legal system started to develop through the early part of the twentieth century, up until the early 1950s. However, during the Cultural Revolution, most existing laws were abandoned and the legal system was demolished with the

Resolution Gone Wrong

A few years ago, we were involved with a UK multinational corporation that had been working with a large state-owned enterprise (SOE) in western regional China. It was seeking the recovery of funds it had pre-paid for manufacturing expenses to the SOE and its subsidiary. The money had been siphoned off and the goods, never manufactured. The subsidiary was subsequently closed down, and its operations were relocated to another subsidiary.

The UK company sought to sue the SOE and its management in China. They had law firms and the British Embassy in Beijing lobbying to resolve the case. The lower court in the regional area heard the case and ruled in the first instance in favor of the UK company against the subsidiary. However, the SOE would not return the money.

The parties appealed at the Provincial Court. They ruled again in favor of the UK company. However, the court said that the legal ruling meant nothing unless the UK company paid another US$50,000 to the court as an enforcement fee.

Well, not surprisingly, our advice was not to pay and instead find a mutually trusted party to mediate. But this company decided to throw good money after bad. They paid the court this fee and subsequently, lost it all.

---

introduction of the Marxist belief that the dictatorship of the proletariat should not be regulated by law. Most universities stopped offering legal courses, and lawyers were stripped of their professional credentials and relocated to community farms in the poorer areas of China.

Since the 1970s, China has slowly recovered from this devastation and is doing a remarkable job in re-establishing the legal system. With ongoing economic reform and the opening up of the Chinese economy to the West and entry into the World Trade Organization (WTO), changes needed to be made to the legal system to attract suitable international investment and to support a smooth transition. The Chinese government started constructing a working socialist society, introducing and enacting new laws to govern the growing economy and international trade.

The concept of "the rule of law" was written into the Constitution in one of its amendments in 1999. The move was hailed by the then Minister of Justice Zhang Fusen as "an important milestone in China's history of the legal system."[1]

The development of new laws took on a frightening pace through the latter part of the 1990s, with new laws being introduced on a monthly basis.

---

[1] "The Rule of Law Progresses Steadily in China," *China Daily*, November 12, 2002.

The National People's Congress and its standing committee formulated more than 109 new laws (plus over 600 administrative rules and regulations) that now account for 45 percent of China's 242 laws. This translates into ten new major laws per year, creating a massive reinstatement and relearning period for lawyers and business people.

However, one example of the law-lagging life is that China has only now passed legislation on manufacturing regulations for electric bikes; yet these bikes have been on sale in China for the last ten years.

We believe that the still-evolving Chinese legal system has started to take on a maturity that is encouraging to Western business people entering into legal relationships with Chinese enterprises.

A Codified System

The Chinese decided to adopt a codified system that relies heavily on the laws being set out in clear terms in codes and statutes with very few common law or court judgments to provide guidance in interpretation. This is generally known as "black letter law," where laws are in writing and only interpreted by separate ordinances or administrative guidance/regulations. It is similar to the Japanese or German system of laws. However, it is quite different from both the American and British systems, which are based on common law principles developed over many years in a common law court system, which gives way to interpretation of laws by courts and the creation of precedents.

The early fears held by foreigners doing business in China about the emerging legal system have not been realized. A proper legal system is taking shape, and dispute resolution has reached a relatively mature stage. The court system, while still somewhat fragile, does attempt to dispense justice fairly and properly, although as with all legal systems, those with the deepest pockets appear to have the best chance of a favorable outcome.

Court Actions/Legal Cases

Given the rapid expansion of the legal system, and the new laws being introduced on a monthly basis, things can get chaotic in the development of a legal case and getting a fair hearing. The Chinese legal system reportedly processes around eight million cases annually—almost 31,000 cases per day.

The number of intellectual property rights (IPR) cases has increased in recent years. Between 2002 and 2006, Chinese courts concluded 52,437 IPR civil cases.[2]

---

[2] "Legal system offers 'due protection'," *China Daily*, 25 April 2007.

It is argued (not convincingly) that this rapid increase in legal action reflects the rapid development of IPR protection in China. However, in our opinion, it merely represents the local business community becoming more aware of their legal rights related to intellectual property. While this will assist IPR protection, it still does not represent satisfactory law development.

More Lawyers?

Undoubtedly, China is one of the few countries in the world that needs more lawyers. The profession was wiped out during the Cultural Revolution and no legal courses were offered in universities from 1958 onward until the late 1970s. Therefore, today, the most senior and qualified lawyers in law firms across China are only in their mid-40s.

By 2005, China had approximately 118,000 lawyers (up from only 40,000 in the early 1990s) and 11,691 law firms. Most of them are located in the coastal region, particularly in Beijing, Shanghai, Guangzhou, and Shenzhen. More than 200 counties in remote areas do not have lawyers.

Despite the recent improvements, China's lawyers are still busy honing their skills, particularly with regard to facing the new challenges brought about by China's membership in the WTO and its pledge to further open up its legal services market. As in many other countries, a competent and good lawyer is difficult to find. The language barrier makes it even more difficult for a foreign business to identify a suitable legal counsel or a lawyer. However, it is possible to find a good lawyer when you know where to look and who to ask for recommendations.

Foreign Legal "Invasion"

For the past ten years, there has been a slow opening up of the market to allow international legal firms to establish themselves in China. The Ministry of Justice has begun to license law firms from around the world. Although there is a limit to the number of firms that can be approved from each country, hundreds of foreign law firms in China now represent the extensive list of nations actively trading there.

However, care should be taken when dealing with these firms. They are only able to practice the law of the home jurisdiction in which they have been admitted. On most occasions, if there is a need for a "sign off" from a Chinese lawyer, an international law firm will be required to get a local law firm to work with the foreign firm.

Unfortunately, this leads to an increase in both legal fees and also the time required to get sensible, practical advice. If, after careful consideration, you do decide to work with an international law firm, make sure that you know and are happy with the Chinese partner it engages.

China has modeled the opening up of its legal profession to the world after Japan. It is restrictive and very protective of its rapidly developing local legal profession. Most local legal firms have limited experience and offer inconsistent quality of service when dealing with complex cross-border transactions. We recommend careful due diligence and establishing long-term relationships with reputable local firms. These firms can be sourced through your embassy, trade association, or Chamber of Commerce in the local community. Be mindful of their strengths and weaknesses—certain legal skills can be lacking in local firms and you can experience patchy professionalism. Take time to choose the right legal provider.

Dispute Resolution

The Chinese legal system has also been enhanced with an alternative dispute resolution system. This system developed from normal Western principles of dispute resolution; it arbitrates and/or mediates disputes between parties and is enforceable by law.

The most active arbitration organization in China is the China International Economic and Trade Arbitration Commission (CIETAC), in operation for more than fifty years. Since 2000, the CIETAC has also been known as the Arbitration Court of the China Chamber of International Commerce (CCOIC). The CIETAC website states that it accepts both domestic and international cases. More than 700 cases are filed each year, most of them international.

However, difficulties still exist within the system, and arbitration decisions granted overseas can be difficult, if not impossible, to enforce in China. A judgment in your favor in your own country will have little effect.

For example, when a contract is breached, you will need to ascertain that your contract conforms to the Chinese law and is fully enforceable in China. You will have to sue for a breach of contract in China. The Chinese law actually does provide powerful contractual remedies to deal with the most potential business disputes. However, if your contract does not take advantage of these provisions, those remedies will be unavailable.

"We Have Already Agreed" Versus "Legally Binding"

The Chinese view of contracts and the signing of documents is entirely different from the Western view. A foreigner must always take care when forming a view of the state of negotiations, even when one enters into a legally-binding agreement. While a deal can be struck and the crucial terms can be agreed upon, reducing the agreement to writing is not an important aspect of the Chinese approach to business. In the West, the contract is the end of the negotiations and the beginning of a legal relationship. The Chinese, however, may regard the contract as the beginning of the negotiation. A lot depends on what experience the Chinese party has had in dealing with international companies and whether the transaction was an international, rather than a purely domestic one.

The Chinese don't really appreciate that a signed contract is legally binding. It is often approached as a mere formality. They do not inherently trust or rely on the contract, particularly in the case of intimate business dealings. It is crucial to communicate to your Chinese partner how important the contract terms are to you, and make sure the message is delivered precisely.

It is also vital to ensure that the final contract is properly stated in Chinese, and not simply in your own language. One of the most common legal traps is the dual language contract. Remember that the Chinese law dictates that the only enforceable contract is the one in Chinese. All too often,

Water can Keep a Boat Afloat, or Sink It

There are many non-litigious ways in which the Chinese settle disputes. One of our Chinese friends is a successful entrepreneur in China. We share a particular difficult dispute he had with a competitor.

He used to run an online shopping portal in Beijing. The website serves as a shopping mall for both business and individual customers. The website was "advertising" without paying by using a technique that created a "popup" web link window on Baidu—the most popular search engine in China.

When Baidu heard of this, they took their own action instead of contacting lawyers. Within minutes, Baidu directed millions of their hits to the company's portal—which instantly crashed the server.

Our friend was in a dilemma. He could not seek legal help as that would take months and would affect his business. He was losing money by the minute.

He asked some of his media friends for help. They put a by-line on a news strip on one of the popular business TV channels that night to say that "a famous search engine was directing traffic to an online shopping website with the intention of interrupting its operations." At the same time, he asked a mutual friend to mediate by apologizing to Baidu for what his company had done.

After an intense twenty-four hours, the dispute was resolved in a Chinese way. Baidu accepted the apology via the mutually respected friend, our friend's portal went back online, and his company agreed to pay and advertise on Baidu immediately.

the Chinese version is different in many respects. We have seen many cases where this has proven to be costly.

In such circumstances, the parties' legal rights become tenuous and dispute resolution becomes difficult. A clear understanding of the Chinese approach, combined with legal protection wherever appropriate, can not only save time and money but also provide a satisfactory solution for both parties.

Mutual Friends Can Help

Using mutual friends to solve disputes between parties is a very common Chinese way of resolving difficulties and is a prime example of how the Chinese believe that they are all connected and must act accordingly. In many disputes, commercial or otherwise, it is better to convey a message

---

The Intermediation

A married couple (Sue, a Chinese overseas returnee and John, a foreigner working in Beijing) went into a 50/50 partnership with a local Chinese couple (Cindy and David, a local Chinese businessman) in 2004, through the introduction of a mutual friend, Ray. Sue and David (a local Chinese businessman) were actively involved in the operations while John and Cindy were non-executive directors.

In less than a year, the differences between the partners became painfully obvious. Both parties were thinking of ending the business relationship. As the dispute reached its peak, David arranged for the office equipment to be secretly taken away, as hostage for expenses. John and Cindy subsequently acted as "mediators" and did their best to dissolve the partnership amicably. In a series of structured meetings, they discussed issues in a civil manner, until they realized that Sue and David were never going to arrive at an agreement. The anger ran deep in both the parties.

Left with little choice and no stomach for lawyers or litigation, they turned to their mutual friend, Ray, who had originally introduced them to each other. Ray had separate conversations with each couple over meals, in an attempt to mediate. At first, he worked diligently to stop them from going their separate ways. Failing to do so, he had a second round of meals and phone calls, seeking to help the partners reach an amicable solution to end the business.

Unfortunately it did not work, as both couples thought the other party was always demanding too much. Eventually, Ray gave up being the mediator. Even at the time of writing, the dispute is unresolved and the business is stalemated. Ray is still doing his best to bring the parties together, but has not been successful so far.

through a mutually concerned partner or mutual friend in a circuitous route rather than dealing with the dispute in a confrontational manner.

Not surprisingly, the mutual friend may be the person who brokered the introduction between the disputing parties during happier times. That person has a moral, and sometimes vested, interest in helping resolve the dispute. The introducer (mutual friend) in any introduction usually knows that he or she may be called upon to act as a mediator.

Aversion to Conflict

The Chinese aversion to legal conflict is actually an aversion to conflict in general. Most Chinese tend to avoid argument and disagreements at all cost. That does not mean there aren't occasional explosions of anger or tension.

What happened in our apartment building compound gives a good insight into how a civil dispute can be handled. In a Western environment,

Real Life Dramas

We live in one of the major exclusive compounds in Beijing. One day we noticed a black Rolls Royce chained up near the entrance of the underground car park. Apparently, the building managers had decided to take the law into their own hands to resolve a dispute they had with the car owner.

One of the wealthy residents called in his own thugs. Some twenty of them tried to free the car, scuffling with twenty apartment security guards. The police were called and two police cars were stationed outside the gate for the rest of that day. The apartment management hired black-suited professional bodyguards—the rationale being that if any of the "temporary professionals" hurt one of the thugs, the management company could not be blamed or sued.

With security guards swarming around, thugs on the outside, police at the gate, and bodyguards with their earpieces watching everyone, more and more residents started to pay attention and wondered what was going on. The scene was set for an embarrassing stand-off. Residents were forced to avoid the picket lines and go around to a side gate. No one was allowed into the complex without showing proof of identity.

After a few more hours of jostling, it all came to nothing. The law was met by similar strength and the petulant resident merely wanted to embarrass the building management into submission. The police took no action as there was no serious violence involved. The Rolls Royce remained chained for many days following this incident until one day it was quietly removed by the owner, after a private settlement of the dispute.

this type of dispute would have found its way into a lower court of law as a debt collection action. In China (even in Beijing, which is the most law-abiding city in China), it was settled outside the legal system.

INTO THE ABYSS

The quote at the beginning of this chapter—"Make the big things small and the small things go away"—is a beautiful Chinese dispute resolution ethos where in a major dispute, it is best to set about doing exactly that. To help you understand its real meaning, we need to recall one of Geoff's unfortunate close encounters with Chinese conflict.

Geoff's Jeep Story

In early 2004, China was in an unprecedented state of panic as Severe Acute Respiratory Syndrome (SARS) had gripped the nation. Beijing became a war zone. Police were on the streets and public places were closed. People began to desert the city. Restaurants, hotels, theaters, and office buildings were emptied.

Geoff continued to manage his office in Beijing, but decided to send his family back to the relative safety of Sydney. One evening, he joined a few friends in a meal to say farewell to his friend John, who was heading to Shanghai. It was a small gathering, including John and two interracial couples (American husbands and Chinese wives).

After the meal, they adjourned to a popular entertainment district near the Forbidden City, travelling in Geoff's jeep twisting and turning through the narrow Beijing alleyways. He parked in the only remaining space, right outside a popular bar. A furious man appeared in front of the jeep waving his arms, shouting obscenities. The Chinese-speaking friends in the car explained that he was the owner of a Mercedes and that he was accusing Geoff of hitting his car that had been parked (awkwardly) down one of the alleys.

Geoff and John (who speaks passable Mandarin) went to sort out this small misunderstanding. A crowd began to gather and they followed them to the Mercedes.

The car was in the middle of the street and the driver's wife stood at the rear of the car, with folded arms, glaring at Geoff. There was sufficient room to navigate around the Mercedes and drive down the alley. The driver pointed to a small scratch on the corner of the back bumper bar and blamed Geoff for it.

Geoff began to laugh as the tiny mark on the black bumper was white whereas his jeep was blue with silver bull bars. It was certainly not his car that had hit the Mercedes. Geoff couldn't understand why the owner would think that it was.

Unfortunately, laughing was a mistake and clearly showed disrespect. The discussions flowed back and forth (with John as translator) with accusations and counter-accusations. Slowly, a crowd started to gather and nearly sixty Chinese surrounded them, blocking the entire street.

As his wife grew tired, she threatened to call the police! At last, Geoff thought, justice will prevail. But he was wrong!

A policeman on a bike arrived to the cheers of the Chinese onlookers. He examined everyone's papers, and asked Geoff to move his car so it could be examined alongside the Mercedes. After a brief examination, the policeman concluded that it was Geoff's doing.

Geoff was speechless at this rapid and misplaced judgment. He made another mistake thinking he could apply his own sense of justice in these circumstances.

The American friends who had been at the bar with their two Chinese wives came to Geoff's "rescue." The onlookers began to abuse the Chinese wives, calling them traitors and lovers of Western trash. The women were in tears and the crowds started to push and shove.

Then Geoff said that notwithstanding all this talk, the Mercedes was parked illegally. To which the crowd responded, "But you invaded Iraq illegally!"

The (alleged) motor vehicle incident was escalating into an international incident. The policeman almost gave up and tried to convince Geoff that it was best to settle the dispute privately, especially as it was such a minor incident. He rode off saying he would be back in thirty minutes, taking all the registration papers with him.

The Americans reached into their pockets pulling out 100 RMB notes (about US$12 at that time) telling Geoff to give them to the Mercedes owner as this was clearly a waste of time. Geoff threw the money in the hope that this would settle the disagreement as over two hours had passed by then!

The Mercedes driver reached out to accept the money, but his wife refused, saying that money would not resolve the humiliation. In China, you should never throw or shove money (or anything really) at people. It can mean great disrespect or rudeness toward the recipient. Also, this action prompted scorn and abuse from the restless (and somewhat drunken) crowd.

The policeman returned only to learn that all attempts to solve the dispute had failed. He looked in disbelief at the Mercedes driver and fined Geoff. Despite Geoff's protests, he confiscated Geoff's driver's licence and registration papers, and told him to visit the local police station the next day to sort matters out.

(Continued)

(*Continued*)

The crowd began yelling that Geoff was a foreigner and might leave the town, so the policeman should take his car instead. The American friends were jostling and the crowd was cheering; the policeman, fearing he would totally lose control, called for reinforcement and a tow truck.

The crowd cheered and then happily dispersed as Geoff's car was towed away. Geoff stood in the now deserted street tightly gripping his car key, wondering how to get his car back. He took a taxi home, and started to plot out how he could bring the whole weight of the legal system crashing down upon the heads of the perpetrators of this injustice!

Early next morning, he called Helen in Sydney and she was immediately worried. He started hesitantly saying everything was OK, that he had a small motor vehicle incident—but the car was fine! The only small problem was that their newly acquired car was impounded, but there was no reason to be worried as he had a great plan to get it back. It was time to seek help from their powerful friends in the Chinese legal system to see justice being done!

Helen was quiet for a moment after hearing all this. Then she said: "Stop right there. Please forget about going to lawyers and seeking retribution. What you need to do is to make the big things small, and the small things go away."

She told Geoff to contact his personal assistant, who was bilingual and then get their local Chinese driver to go to the police station together. Geoff's "Chinese negotiating team" told him to stay outside the police office. His personal assistant (PA), her husband (who also came along to help), and the driver went inside to see the only senior policeman on duty.

After what seemed like eternity, Geoff peered in through the window. He saw the three of them sitting around the table with the police, as if they were long-time friends. The driver was reading the policeman's newspaper, and the PA's husband was re-programming the policeman's mobile phone. Sensing Geoff's impatience and nervousness, the PA came outside and said that they were discussing some general issues and that there was no need to panic.

Shortly after, they were swapping stories and jokes. After fifteen more minutes, the policeman emerged to say that it was all sorted out and Geoff could have his car back. Obviously, things had gotten out of hand last night, and if they had known Geoff was an Australian, it would not have happened. Sitting in the car that he once thought might be lost forever, Geoff felt a sense of the surreal. He quickly checked the belongings that he'd left in the car. Everything was untouched. While sighing with relief, he wondered what would have happened had he insisted upon the Western way of fighting for justice!

Compensation for damage to the Mercedes still needed to be sorted out with the other driver, and until that happened, the police would keep his license. The Mercedes owner refused to talk to Geoff's driver as that would be regarded as dealing with the wrong class of person. So he got his own driver to call Geoff's driver to come up with a solution.

The insurance company also began to negotiate with the Mercedes driver. They looked at the scratch and offered 1,000 RMB. He demanded 10,000 RMB. After three months, it was eventually settled on 1,000 RMB!

After months of many phone calls between the driver and the insurer, the conflict was finally resolved. Geoff's license was returned, and the Mercedes owner got exactly what he would have received on the night of the incident!

Tips from The Tale of Woe

This tale of woe has taught us the following lessons:

1. Never negotiate in front of an unruly crowd.
2. Don't impose your own sense of justice in a foreign environment.
3. Choose your interpreter carefully—sometimes it works better when you don't have one!
4. Mediate and compromise early. Never let things get out of hand.

Conclusion

The Chinese legal system is seeking a balanced approach that inherits wisdom from traditional Chinese thought and philosophy, while adopting the best from the West. As China continues to attract foreign investment and becomes more integrated with the rest of the world, a more globalized and modern legal system is vital for China to sustain itself.

The Chinese will do almost anything to avoid conflict. However, when pushed into a corner, ugliness can prevail. Beware of mob mentality and stay clear of ugly confrontations. However, when conflict is clearly unavoidable, the best approach is to break the big issue into smaller ones, and handle each smaller issue separately, resolving it one bit at a time.

Chapter 10
Localization and Intellectual Property

Let foreign things serve China
Mao Zedong

Back in 220 AD, China was divided into three kingdoms—Wei, Shu, and Wu. It was a period of power struggles and wars, and many Chinese generals developed creative military strategies.

During this period, Cao Cao, the General of Wei, led his troops into war against the Wu Kingdom. However the Kingdom of Shu sent its chief strategist Zhuge Liang to the Wu Kingdom in the hope of forming an alliance against the advances of General Cao.

However Wu's commander-in-chief, Zhou Yu, was very jealous and suspicious of Zhuge's reputed talents. He challenged Zhuge with a seemingly impossible mission. He asked him to help with the defense of Wu and make 100,000 arrows within ten days.

To his astonishment Zhuge replied: "I only need three days for this."

He secretly borrowed twenty boats and assigned thirty soldiers to each boat. He put thatched roofs and straw figures along the sides. In the wee hours of the third day, as he had correctly predicted, a thick fog rolled in across the water that separated the warring armies.

The little flotilla was pushed out toward Cao's enemy camp. When the flotilla neared Cao's camp, the soldiers were told to beat their drums and cry out, feigning an attack on the enemy's army.

In the thick fog, General Cao ordered his 3,000 archers to shoot their arrows at the approaching enemy boats. In time, Zhuge recovered his twenty boats—which contained more than 100,000 of Cao's arrows!

Throughout China's history, there have been many creative and inspirational people such as Zhuge Liang. China's achievements have been well recorded by western scientists. In his monumental project, *Science and Civilisation in China*, Joseph Needham helped the world to better understand the marvelous history of science and technology in China. In his book *The Man Who Loved China: The Fantastic Story of the Eccentric Scientist Who Unlocked the Mysteries of the Middle Kingdom*, which is based on Joseph Needham's life, Simon Winchester outlines more than 260 Chinese inventions and discoveries identified by Joseph Needham.

Perhaps, more importantly, Needham posed a profound question that is yet to be answered: "Why was it that despite the immense achievements of traditional China, it was in Europe, not China, where the scientific and industrial revolutions occurred?"

Needham was unable to find a satisfactory answer to his own question during his lifetime. In this chapter, we invite you to seek clues that may answer this question by looking at the historical and cultural contexts of intellectual property (IP) in China.

In China, there is a traditional misperception of or a general lack of appreciation for scientific knowledge or innovation in the commonly accepted Western sense. In recent years, this very relaxed Chinese attitude (at times, ignorance) toward IP, compounded by the lack of support from a developed legal structure, has caused a great deal of stress for those within and outside China.

We look at efforts and changes that have been made to date, and also evaluate some of the IP strategies that are most commonly adopted by both international and Chinese companies to provide a framework for protecting and growing your IP.

HISTORICAL CONTEXT

As we know, the Chinese believe that we are all connected. People do their best to live harmoniously with others, as Confucius said: "It is a pleasure to have friends from afar" 有朋自远方来，不亦乐乎 *you peng zi yuanfang lai, bu yi yue hu.*

Indeed, during its long history, even before Needham, China received many foreign friends, Marco Polo perhaps being one of the most famous. Some visitors liked China so much that they decided to stay. During the Han (206 BC–220 AD) and Tang Dynasties (618–906 AD) (the Han-Tang Period), China was the world's economic and scientific superpower, and many foreign traders and visitors settled in China during that period. However, during the last few hundred years, China has lagged behind the West in the quest for industrialization and modernization.

The Development of IP Awareness

From a global perspective, China is following a reasonably standard path similar to other nations that had to develop IP laws and regulations. Many conveniently forget that over 150 years ago, the United States was the world's worst offender for abusing IP rights. At that time, Americans took technological knowledge from Europe to help build a nation and forge a booming economy.

Because of its relative "late awakening" to economic development, China has not yet had the time or opportunity to acquire the refined view of IP that has existed in the West for over a century. At this early stage of rapid economic growth, brand creation and protection are secondary to market share, cost-effectiveness, efficient production, and distribution.

However, as China develops its burgeoning middle class, there will be a rapid change in society's attitudes toward branding and IP. Price and the speed to market will no longer be the sole determining factors for product choice. In fact, the trend is already manifesting in the fast-growing luxury goods market.

Cultural Context

Arguably, traditional Chinese culture does not provide the fertile ground that is necessary for the sustained growth and development of science and technology. Needham himself commented that Confucianism focused on the practical application of technological processes, not on the importance of theoretical investigation. As a result, most Chinese inventions were empirically sophisticated but lacked theoretical documentation.

Another important factor is the hierarchical nature of the society. Traditionally, becoming government officials was regarded as the ultimate achievement for scholars. Therefore, mainstream thinking was that the primary purpose of knowledge is advancing one's political career.

A further reason can be seen in the need to protect face, which is ranked higher than the pursuit of truth. Whenever there was disagreement between a teacher and his disciple, the voice of the teacher was always louder. The authoritative status of certain people will never be challenged openly, even if these same people lack the necessary knowledge.

Both Taoism and Buddhism place an emphasis on personal enlightenment rather than on the indulgence of physical comfort and accumulation of worldly wealth. It is the belief of many Chinese that happiness does not directly correlate to money.

The Chinese View of "Give and Take"

Culturally speaking, it is clear that the Chinese have a very different view of "give and take." This 阴 *yin* and 阳 *yang* attitude is deeply embedded in Chinese minds as two sides of the same coin. Such thinking not only applies to solving problems but also to how the Chinese view sharing knowledge or information (or IP). Successful business owners are able to balance the give and take in such a way that they are always one step ahead of their competitors.

Historically, ancient China has given freely to the world its four great inventions—printing, paper-making, the compass, and gunpowder. The Chinese feel that most inventions or original thoughts had long been known by their talented ancestors—the four mentioned above being the most notable examples. Hence the Chinese saying, "most things are copied from various sources" 天下文章八大抄 *tianxia wenzhang ba da chao*. Of course, such a statement needs to be read in the context and with a Chinese sense of humor (a mixture of midstream thinking, self-irony, and respect for ancestors). Many Chinese criticize "artful plagiarism" and are adamant about the importance of true originality.

Importantly, the Chinese are not really accustomed to protecting their own IP, let alone other's. For example, every Chinese person can quote ancient sayings, but very few know their origin. Entrepreneurs watch and learn from each other all the time in the rush to market, or to keep a lookout on the development of the next new idea.

When one good idea works, there will be copiers the next day. Competition is so fierce that even in clothing stores at local shopping malls, there are signs saying, "Competitors do not enter" to stop the competitors from copying new designs and gathering other competitive information on pricing, sales, and marketing techniques.

How the Chinese View Branding

Clearly, there is a lack of knowledge in China about branding and the value of IP. The Chinese find it difficult to put a monetary value on the intangible nature of services and brands.

For example, international professional service companies faced tremendous challenges when they first established their operations in China. Often the Chinese are keen to get free advice and shy away from paying consulting fees, thinking that their combined actions and thoughts will always equal any new or smart idea. There is a saying that best translates as, "Three cobblers with their wits combined, equal Zhuge Liang the master mind" 三个臭皮匠，抵个诸葛亮 *sange chou pijiang, dige zhugeliang*.[1]

As a result of this belief that ordinary people can be as wise as the experts, it took consulting firms a number of years to gain momentum and expand in China.

---

[1] This saying was translated by Qian Zhongshu (1910–1999), a renowned Chinese scholar and author. Zhuge Liang (Kong Ming) was a brilliant strategist, inventor, and scholar who lived during the Three Kingdoms Era in China (181–234 AD).

Another well-known challenge that China continues to grapple with is counterfeiting. Even the government's new IP laws struggle to treat the various symptoms effectively. In general, many small and mediocre businesses direct their energy toward copying and conforming, rather than toward creating their own brands or products and services.

Were one to argue that there is a single positive effect of counterfeiting, undoubtedly, it would be that the counterfeit marketing of global brands has provided these brands with a significant early mover advantage.

To fully appreciate this view, it is important to look at the (brief) history of luxury brands in China. For a long time, most Chinese wore blue Mao suits or uniforms. The French fashion designer, Pierre Cardin, visited China in 1979 when the reforms had started. In the following fifteen years, he made twenty visits to China. The Chinese regarded Pierre Cardin as the number one (or the only) international brand in clothing. His brand was synonymous with high quality clothes and luxury goods.

Helen recalls that even in the early 1990s, there were a few international luxury consumer brands in the China market. In Beijing, they were found mostly in the very few five-star hotels that most Chinese would not dare enter. Most Chinese consumers learned about the brands by window shopping at markets such as the Silk Market.[2] In their view, the brands worth copying had to be internationally famous!

A large percentage of customers who bought a fake at a small fraction of the cost of the real thing are now in a position to purchase the genuine brand. Invariably, they remember the earlier generation of copies and are now loyal customers. Brands that were not counterfeited now have to invest significant amounts of money to achieve the same level of market exposure and loyalty.

First Mover Advantage

A Chinese friend of ours runs a very successful children's clothing brand management and distribution business headquartered in Beijing. He has the exclusive license for China on all his brands from the United States, and their prices have always been at least 50 percent higher than those of his local competitors. Marketing through premium general store chains and other high-end channels, sales of his children's clothing have been number one in most major Chinese cities (including Beijing and Shanghai) for a number of years.

His view of counterfeiting is that the first generation of counterfeits actually helped those international brands gain first mover advantage.

---

[2] The Silk Market is one of the most popular market places in Beijing, and a regular stop for tourists. In the four-storey building, one can easily find Chinese tableclothes, fake Gucci sunglasses, fake Prada bags, and hundreds of stands selling counterfeit clothes and watches.

> ### Silk Market Sued
>
> A close Chinese friend in the legal profession specializes in trademark and IP law. A few years ago, she represented four of the world's leading luxury brands in suing the management of the Silk Market shopping center for allowing counterfeits of their bags, sunglasses, watches, and clothes to be sold by shopping center owners.
>
> In this high-profile case, the court ruled in favor of the four international brands. The management of the market was ordered to stop these activities immediately and pay a fine of RMB 10,000 (equivalent to approximately US$1,200) to each of the luxury brand companies as compensation. While we agree that such a small commercial penalty imposed upon the offenders was a token gesture, it was at least a good start!

THREE-AND-A-HALF CHINESE LOCALIZATION MODELS

To sum up how the Chinese localize foreign ideas and products, we recommend three-and-a-half schools of thought as a guide. The three mainstream approaches are:

- Accept and preserve everything;
- Localize with some Chinese flavor;
- Take only the foreign flavor.

Model 1: The "Yiwu" Model (Accept and Preserve)

Yiwu, a small town in southern China, approximately 300 kilometres southwest of Shanghai, is the largest small commodities market in the world. Yiwu boasts over 300,000 products ranging from socks, fashion accessories, and Christmas tree lights, to hardware, electrical sockets, and windshield wiper covers.

More than 200,000 traders and 8,000 foreign businessmen—from over 100 different countries and territories—have permanently set up shops in the city. Among the most noticeable are Muslim traders who have managed to establish a thoroughly pan-Islamic Chinese life.

Middle Eastern Muslim traders buy about 75 per cent of the 1,000 containers that leave Yiwu each day. Recently, they have established more than 3,000 permanent offices in the city. The Chinese have supported the "settlement" of these Middle Eastern traders, and encouraged these new "migrants" to extend their culture to the Chinese residents.

The Chinese Muslim Community

Another example is the formation of one of the largest ethnic minorities—the Hui Chinese. Their ancestors were Middle Eastern traders who first traveled to China along the Silk Road during the Tang Dynasty. During the next 1,100 years, their descendants and converts became Hui Chinese, the largest group of China's Muslims.

Over many generations, they intermarried with the Han Chinese, and adopted Mandarin as a common language. The Hui Chinese are dispersed throughout China. There is a sense of community in each city, as they worship at their own mosque and generally live in the same area.

Helen only realized that one of her high school classmates was Hui Chinese when there were festive celebrations at school and dumplings were prepared. The teacher always prepared non-pork fillings for him.

The following lines from an article illustrates the harmony seen in Yiwu.

> At day's end, the muezzin's call reaches out from Yiwu's first mosque in the Hong Lou Hotel, past the front desk, to the workers waiting with paint rollers by the steps. Green matting is rolled out across the parking lot as an overflowing crowd kneels beneath the setting sun. Behind them a Chinese couple volleys a badminton shuttle, totally unfazed.... A Uighur boy roasts kebabs beneath a single, bare bulb.
>
> And Afghan traders, late from the market, hurry back into the womb of Yiwu's Arabian Nights.[3]

Model 2: The "Foreign Things Serve China" Model (Localize with Chinese Flavor)

Mao promoted this idea, and the most notable disciple of it was Deng Xiaoping. In 1978, Deng visited Singapore to study its state model. Soon afterward, he commented on how Singapore successfully used foreign investment for its economic growth. He then established Chinese policies to welcome foreign investment, doing his best to localize the lessons he learnt from Singapore. Deng also visited Japan twice, during 1978 and 1979, with the clear objective of studying the "Japanese model."

---

[3] Based on "How a Quaint City in Southern China bridges trade between Muslims and Chinese," *China Economic Review*, September 2007 <www.chinaeconomicreview.com/cer/2007_09/Culture_and_commerce.html>

Following this new "open door policy," many Chinese SOEs started to form joint ventures, and/or to start overseas operations. The most successful early examples are Japanese-invested joint ventures, largely due to Deng's meetings with both political and business leaders while visiting Japan. While the Japanese companies enjoyed many years of financial rewards and market dominance in China, the Chinese were pleased to learn and develop ways to localize and use this success to their own advantage.

This was a very challenging journey for the many parties involved, including the Chinese government and its related agencies. Maintaining a balance between encouraging international investment while learning from it to build a local industry capable of competing globally has been a difficult road. Needless to say, there were and will be businesses that make it and those that don't.

Model 3: The "Just Take It" Model (Take Only the Foreign Flavor)

You may recall Lu Xun, who wrote the famous Ah Q story on face (面子 *mianzi*). He wrote another essay, "Taking Things from Outside China", and popularized the saying 拿来主义 *nalai zhuyi*, loosely translated as "just take it."

Unfortunately, groups of Chinese in the business community have adopted this model as their business strategy. With China's extremely fierce domestic competition, when someone has a good idea, it is rapidly followed by either a copy or an improvement. So far, China has thrived on this continual "develop–copy–refine" cycle.

As the market and business environment is relatively immature, many Chinese view short-term survival and profitability as their primary concerns and are yet to realize or sustain the value of their brands or ideas. It is simply a race to the market to produce the most attractive product at the cheapest cost. However, that is slowly changing as the government, and increasingly, the entrepreneurs as well, promote the move from China as the "world factory" to China as the "world's laboratory." They are realizing that

> ### *A Chinese Californian Restaurant*
>
> A few years ago, a famous fast food chain in Beijing, Californian Beef Noodle Restaurant, enjoyed great success as many Chinese diners thought that they were eating at an American restaurant.
>
> Even Helen thought that it was a chain opened by the same company from California, until an American friend told her that such a chain does not exist in the United States!

the old "copy/just take it" model will not work as the market becomes more sophisticated and integrated.

The Half Model: Imitation-Inspired Innovation—The Spirit of 山寨 *Shanzai*

This "just take it" model has recently evolved into a major new sub-culture of creativity and innovation—the shanzai phenomenon.

The word shanzai was originally used to describe fake or brandless cell phones. Manufactured by unauthorized and small-scale factories on the Southeast coast of China, they now have an estimated market share of 25 percent of the 830 million mobile phone users in China—the world's largest cell phone market in 2010.

China Central Television conducted a survey on shanzai culture in 2008. This gave national exposure to the word and the associated subculture, sparking a heated domestic debate. The results showed that 50 percent of Chinese netizens support the craze. Western media like *The Wall Street Journal* and *The New Yorker* have reported on the shanzai phenomenon and presented it as a form of rebellion and resistance to mainstream culture.

Many may not realize that the Chinese naturally associate shanzai with the story of Song Jiang and other Liangshan ancient heroes. Most Chinese know about these heroes and their fascinating adventures through study at school, listening to stories told to them by family members, or reading the 14th century classic *Water Margin* (水浒传 *shuihuzhuan*), one of the four great classical novels in Chinese literature. The book describes Song Jiang, a Chinese Robin Hood. He and his followers fought and defeated the Emperor's troops, and lived in a mountain fortress. It has also been made into a hugely popular TV series in Mainland China on more than one occasion. The word shanzai also has the implied meaning of challenging corrupt authorities and seeking justice for the weak and common people.

While many Chinese have expressed their concerns about shanzai being a shameless act of piracy or a purely profit-oriented operation, supporters, however, define a shanzai manufacturer as "a vendor who operates a business without observing the traditional rules or practices, often resulting in innovative and unusual products or business models."

The earlier, better-known fake garments, watches, bags, and shoes are not called shanzai products, perhaps because these fake products came into existence before the fake cell phones and never used the term shanzhai.

Originally, the primary market for most shanzai products comprised the price-sensitive consumers. Shanzai phones, for example, enable people with less spending power to access products and services that they would have not have otherwise been able to afford.

In China, there are over 900 million farmers. Although their living standards are improving constantly, their spending power is much lower than that of the same demographic of a developed country. Without shanzai cell phones, China probably would not have so many cell phone users.

The other fan group demographic is the young Chinese, who think that it is cool to have a shanzai cell phone, game player, or MP4. They like these shanzai products because they are creative, and because there is an element of humor and 恶搞 *kuso* (outrageous fun or reckless doings) and "grassroots-intelligence"—all much appreciated by China's youth. Some even collect and share shanzai designs on the Internet, linking shanzai with fun and the "China cool" factor.

Obama Has His Blackberry, I Have My Blockberry!

One can see why shanzai phones have captured a large market share. Not only do they look trendy—similar to popular phones like iPhone (iOrange) or BlackBerry (Blockberry)—but also they have many more useful functions than the original. For example, many offer extra-long standby time of up to one month, dual SIM card support, quadruple cameras and speakers, radio, GPS, touch screen, extra large screen, handwriting recognition, and compatibility with all types of media files. Some even have localized functions that are China-specific, such as an in-built ultraviolet laser for testing counterfeit bank notes.

One of the most recent popular shanzai inventions is called an "Apple Peel." Costing US$60, it wraps around an iTouch and cleverly converts it into an iPhone. The company that launched the product in late 2010 claims that they are not copycats and that they don't make fake products, merely spin offs!

However, poor quality shanzai products may cause injury (mobile phones with unsafe batteries, for example). Fakes or clones of branded products that infringe on IP need to be curbed. Too many copycats hinder the progress of China moving from "made in China" to "created in China." But is imitation a crime? Particularly when the process of imitation also involves innovation.

It is well known that Picasso drew his inspiration from famous Impressionist artists. The similarities are obvious, so much so that there was an exhibition called "Picasso and Masters" held during 2008 and 2009 in Paris. Everyone saw the striking similarity between his paintings and the originals. Had Picasso been born in modern day China, he might have been called a shanzai artist!

But for how long will this shanzai phenomenon last? As Buckminster Fuller, one of the most original thinkers of the twentieth century once said, "You never change things by fighting existing reality. To change something, build a new model that makes the existing model obsolete." In a country where things change constantly, and subcultures emerge and disappear all the time, we have faith that the millions of Chinese innovators will "build something new."

Would the Chinese Ever Drink Coffee?

Some twenty years ago, an American corporate client was planning to start a coffee shop business in China. Geoff's colleague, a foreign lawyer, listened intently to their localization plans. Being an old China hand with a good understanding of Chinese culture, he felt that in a country with a tea-drinking culture thousands of years old, no one would pay to drink bitter coffee, let alone pay US$4 for a cup when a pot of green tea costs less than fifty cents!

His client, however, did not listen to his advice. They started a coffee business joint venture with a local partner in Beijing. That was the beginning of Starbucks in China!

A Chinese "Italian Café"

Starbucks created a new market previously thought to be non-existent in China. It has successfully set a standard in selling coffee culture the American way. It is not surprising to learn that many local brands have emerged, some clearly copying Starbucks.

In the rush to be part of the new market, the Chinese have created odd businesses and bizarre products. A few successful coffee shop chains have developed alongside Starbucks in a very Chinese tradition. They have little to do with coffee apart from creating the atmosphere of a café. They also sell food for the local market, mixing Western and traditional Chinese cuisines.

The Chinese frequent these places to discuss business in private or have meetings with friends while having a meal. Some may order a coffee. However, it is regarded as a fashionable "in" thing to do rather than expressing a genuine thirst for the taste or aroma. Most would still order a green tea instead—even though it costs far more than fifty cents!

Recently, other very "Chinese" café bars have opened, calling themselves "Italian" coffee shops. They sell anything from Brazilian coffee to American products to "invented" Italian coffee or gelato. They typically decorate the store in garish colors with velvet drapes and chandeliers—their idea of "Italian" style. Some even sell beverages called "coffee-tea"—a blend of both!

However as more and more Chinese travel overseas and get a taste of what Italian style really is, they increasingly demand a more authentic experience. Coupled with the demand of the ever-growing numbers of foreign visitors in China, successful foreign-run Italian restaurants have already emerged.

An example is Massimo Masili. The owner of L'Isola (a very successful Italian restaurant in Beijing), opened an Italian café bar close to his restaurant in Beijing. When he first started his small operation a few years ago, it had all the friendliness and style that was typically Italian—quality food, a careful selection of Italian wine with an Italian flair, and so on. It was crammed and had patrons staying until midnight. Mr Masili now has three other bustling branches of his café in Beijing.

It seems that today, any copy of an Italian, American, or any other foreign service brand for that matter, has to live up to standards that would be acceptable to both local and foreign visitors.

Paradigm Shift: From a World Factory to a World Laboratory

No doubt the Chinese government is keenly aware that concerns about IP rights have hindered the further development of China. It is making a continued effort to show its determination to combat IP rights infringements to maintain and attract more foreign investment.

As an example, the government has been publicly burning pirated DVDs and books for years. Also, for the first time, in January 2011, the Chinese minister of commerce invited senior foreign executives to attend a forum and start a conversation on IP rights. Even though some believe that such moves are merely window dressing, it demonstrates the willingness of the government to take action.

We should also remember that China has another ambitious goal—to evolve from today's world factory into tomorrow's world laboratory. To do so requires more than a slogan. Apart from government policies, subsidies, and investments, the traditional thinking that hinders creativity and innovation has to change, and there has to be a system in place to protect the IP rights generated by this future laboratory.

Emerging Scientific Superpower

The need to protect Chinese-owned IP rights is growing rapidly. Some commentators are forecasting that the rise of China, India, and South Korea will reshape the global innovation landscape. Some even warn that the US and European pre-eminence in scientific innovation can no longer be taken for granted.

Since the early 1950s, Mao Zedong was very keen for China to assert its power in the form of scientific development. Back then, that development centered on nuclear power and the development of the A–bomb. However, scientific advancement is now being pursued with the greatest effort.

Fortunately, with the rapid advancement of technology, there is an emerging opportunity for China to leapfrog the legacy systems and conventional thinking that have constrained some of the developed countries. A prime example is that in 2010, China emerged as the world's largest clean technology investor. Significant investment from both government and private sectors has been put into developing environmentally friendly futuristic solutions to overcome the pollution problem while sustaining growth and improving the standard of living.

If you visit a local village, you may come across salesmen on their bicycles promoting solar powered hot water systems to the farmers. A standard solar powered hot water system costs around US$30–50, including installation and one year warranty. The government subsidizes the farmers around $15 for such installation.

As scientific development gains greater momentum, the need for China to protect its own scientific developments and IP will become overwhelming.

Rush to Research and Development (R&D)

Conversely, there are encouraging movements of global companies establishing or expanding their R&D facilities in China. By 2009, more than 1,000 foreign companies had set up R&D centers in China, including Microsoft, IBM, Lucent, Hewlett-Packard, Samsung, Philips, Motorola, and Nokia.

In early 2009, Bayer, the German drug and chemical giant, announced that it would invest 100 million euros in the next five years in Beijing to build the world's fourth largest R&D center.

Unilever launched its sixth global R&D center with a 50 million euro investment in late 2009. The center employs more than 400 research staff members from fifteen countries.

In the automotive industry, the world's largest carmaker, Toyota Motor Corp, plans to strengthen its research and development capabilities in China. Japan's *Nikkei Business Daily* reported in January 2010 that Toyota plans to spend $330 to $440 million to establish an R&D center in Shanghai as early as 2011.

Other global automakers, including Volkswagen AG, General Motors, and Hyundai Corporation, have set up R&D centers in China. Japan's Nissan and Honda also have R&D facilities under their Chinese joint ventures.

Admittedly, most regard the R&D centers as an important part of their localization strategy; it also indicates that many companies are no longer seriously concerned about the drawbacks of China's IP protection.

Going Global

As discussed, rapid economic development and the urge for China to go global are challenging long-held attitudes. Some of China's largest companies are now some of the largest companies in the world. For example, the share value of PetroChina, China's massive (partly state owned) oil and gas company, increased to such a level in 2007 that its market capitalization topped US$1 trillion—the first listed company in the world to do so. PetroChina is now one of world's largest listed companies by market capital.

China has some of the biggest banks, insurance companies, telecommunications carriers, and airlines by market capitalization. It is no surprise that these massive companies want to support their brands and IP rights. The Chinese government, holding a great deal of the value in these companies, will want to protect that value and ensure that suitable laws that provide protection are put in place.

As the Chinese companies seek to compete in the West, they will also have to learn to protect their brands and IP in the fiercely competitive global markets. They will be forced to come to terms with international regulations, and they will naturally seek to influence and encourage similar protection in the domestic market.

Meanwhile, global events like the 2008 Beijing Olympics and the 2010 Shanghai Expo crystallized and focused the government's view on IP rights. Investment related to the Beijing Olympics was estimated to have topped US$30 billion. The government had posted a specific IPR protection white paper dated January 2007 on the official Shanghai Expo website.

As China is rapidly becoming a hotbed for R&D and developing its own brands, it will not only need to improve measures to protect international IP but also domestic IP and brands.

In March 2011, the Chinese government endorsed the 12th Five-Year Plan that set the course for the country's economic and social development until 2015. A key focus is to nurture China's own creative industries and Chinese-business-owned IP assets. Such focus requires strong IP protection structures.

How Foreign Businesses Localize

So what can international companies do? When a foreign company enters the Chinese market, localization and IP become vital issues.

China is a diverse market. Its dramatic geographic disparity requires an initial question to be asked by any company: "What would be the best location to start operations?" Then comes an equally important question: "How much of my business do I have to change to be successful in China?" Many companies succeed by sticking to their own tried-and-true operational methods. Others are forced to modify these methods.

Attention to what works in China and what does not is key to success, but discovering this can be painstaking and expensive. It may mean as little as adapting your logo to Chinese—to as much as substantially modifying your business model.

THREE LOCALIZATION APPROACHES

For Western businesses operating in China, most localization strategies fall into three broad categories:

1. **Stay foreign and unique.** The best example is Starbucks. Note that the underlying success factor for Starbucks is not merely their products; it is the image and culture they cleverly created and promoted. There used to be a popular statement among young Chinese white collar workers—"If I am not in the office, I am either on my way to Starbucks or I am at Starbucks." One can succeed using this model if one is a ground-breaker, a trend leader, and a provider of a product or service embraced by Chinese thinking.
2. **Modify significantly to suit the local conditions.** This may mean that a company's products or services require a major modification in company operations to compete and function in the local market due to regulation (or other constraints). Banks and other service industries fit into this category. The only distinguishing feature or link the China operation may have with the parent business may be branding, trademark, or logo.
3. **Modify operations slightly.** This is necessary for a significant proportion of businesses. Notable success stories include McDonalds and KFC. Both chains, while maintaining global uniformity, also offer local dishes to cater to the different Chinese palate.

SEVEN WAYS TO PROTECT IP

When it comes to protecting your IP, we suggest using all the usual precautions to secure legal entitlements to IP. This includes registering trademarks, designs, or patents, and ensuring that they are not only protected everywhere in China but also worldwide.

It may be necessary to register a company in China to hold the rights and secure the company or product name. While working on this, we strongly encourage seeking appropriate legal and business advice from advisors within China.

We have observed various IP protection strategies that have been adopted—some successful and some less so. We share seven of these below.

The "I Will Sue" Model

This strategy was adopted by leading global luxury brands like Louis Vuitton and Gucci. These companies enforced their IP rights against the fashion counterfeiters and sued the management of the Silk Market in Beijing referred to earlier. While taking action under the Chinese law is an expensive option and must be consistently applied so as to serve its intended purpose, it does send strong and clear signals to the marketplace on what could happen to those who manufacture pirated versions of a well-known international brand.

Many international companies now embrace this strategy. For example, Starbucks won a high-profile case in 2007 against a Shanghai coffee chain using a similar Chinese name and a deceptively similar logo.

The Black Box Model

This strategy protects IP rights by containing or concealing the elements of a product. For example, when a product is manufactured in China, the firm can retain a vital piece of IP by manufacturing one or more elements offshore in a contained environment. Secrecy is maintained with regard to the key parts of the manufacturing process or the product itself.

This strategy can also be modified to have the components of a product manufactured by a number of different manufacturers across China. This circumvents conspiracy to copy the product, and only segments can be counterfeited.

Should you adopt this strategy, it is vital to make sure that your IP rights are secure, and are treated as an integral part of the business. While adequate protection can be provided by independent legal advisors acting on your behalf, when IP rights are key to your business and clearly vulnerable in China, they should always be overseen by key executives.

The Microsoft Model

The Microsoft strategy allowed pirates to copy its software (perhaps involuntarily), and roll it out across China, which set a standard for all PCs. The strategy forgoes early profits by seizing the market and developing a dependent user base.

This has worked to a degree, but relies heavily on solutions that either convert the pirate users to paying users by forcing them to install further upgrades, or being able to track illegal users so as to penalize them in the future.

As the IT industry evolves rapidly, other operating systems could develop—one copy is Foxmail, a competitor to Outlook that operates in a very similar manner. However, as long as Microsoft can stay one step ahead of other industry players, it will continue to survive and prosper in China.

The McDonald's Model

McDonald's chose to roll out its stores across China as company-owned stores (not franchises) to maintain control of its brand and systems. This enabled them to ensure product quality in a food and beverage industry that previously did not have a great deal of experience in this style of handling food. It had to ensure product supply and suitably trained labor to maintain its normal high standards.

Only after more than a decade of being in China did McDonald's feel confident enough to begin franchising stores and move away from the company-owned-stores model.

The Parallel Model

An unusual strategy involves becoming a pirate yourself! For example, the Chinese production company of a recent blockbuster movie was so worried about pirated DVDs that they chose to produce their own pirated version and released the genuine DVD at the same time.

While it is an interesting Chinese strategy, it is not often used, is somewhat risky, and is not applicable to all products.

The Quality Will Prevail Model

When you consistently offer high-standard products, ones that cannot be copied readily, quality will prevail, notwithstanding the cheaper products.

This is applicable to technologically advanced products, for example, motor vehicles such as Mercedes and BMW that cannot be easily copied as well as to a basic paint roller.

A German friend established and operated a factory in China producing German-designed high-quality paint rollers that are priced much higher than the local rollers. While everyone thought he was crazy, the company very quickly secured a healthy market share. It grew exponentially and continues to be a success today as it maintains its high quality.

The Do Nothing Model

This unlikely strategy unfortunately remains the most popular. It is almost doomed to failure and may succeed only when there is a limited market for your product or service.

We have discussed only seven strategies; there are many more to be adopted. Many of the seven above can be combined, depending upon the circumstances. While there may be problems in protecting your IP in China, many companies have found ways to overcome the challenges and prosper in this booming economy. Therefore, while important, IP protection should not be used as an excuse for failing to do business in China.

CONCLUSION

China is a large diverse market with a unique cultural and historic background. The Chinese have a very different view toward IP and branding.

As globalization and the rise of China continues, the need to protect one's IP and brand increase accordingly. As the Chinese economy further develops, more and more Chinese will have a better appreciation of the topic. The Chinese government continues its efforts to improve its measures and actions. IP laws do exist and will often provide protection for your IP and brands.

However, the Chinese market moves quickly and is extremely competitive. It is best to carefully develop a tailored localization strategy based upon one's own products or services, but never varying from one's core competence. Furthermore, a carefully designed IP strategy is a must for China. Otherwise, you will be shanzai'ed before you know it!

Chapter 11 Conclusion

Success depends upon finding harmony between time, place, and people

During the process of writing this book, we were constantly humbled by China—its remarkable history and culture, the tremendous wisdom, and most of all, its amazing people. Even though the book is our best endeavour to capture how the Chinese think and where they come from, we are fully aware that we have only touched the surface, the tip of the China iceberg. By no means, do we claim that this book provides all the clues to deciphering the Chinese minds.

Even today, we continue to gain fascinating insights. As an old Chinese saying goes, "You need to throw a brick first to attract people's jade" 抛砖引玉—*paozhuan yinyu*—someone needs to start a conversation by being the first commentator. So by offering our "brick" in the form of this book, we hope that more people will write in greater detail and cover areas that we may have neglected or merely touched upon.

The rich history of China is very much alive in every Chinese, even though some may not be aware of this legacy. Admittedly, the last thirty years of the "open door" policy have introduced a diverse range of cultural influences into China, exposing the mainland Chinese to a dynamic new world. Although deep down we are all the same and the Chinese are adaptable, they are still conditioned to think, live, and work in ways that are often in sharp contrast to those of the Westerners.

However, what we are witnessing is the great emergence of a nation becoming a global superpower once again. We live in truly exciting times. Never before has the world offered such a stage for celebrating the diverse cultures and uniqueness of each and every one of us. We can choose to live in a global village without losing our own unique identity. Barriers that hindered our older generations no longer exist. The world is flat in many ways and we can visit, re-visit, or live in almost any country we choose. This also means that we have many more opportunities to meet people from other diverse cultures.

How do we navigate the best way forward?

Madame Guan Daosheng, a famous ancient Chinese poet wrote in the 14th century:[1]

Let us take some clay,
Wet it, pat it,
and make an image of you
and an image of me.
Then smash them, crash them,
and with a little water
knead them together.
And out of the new clay we'll remake,
an image of you, and an image of me.
Thus there is a little of you in me,
and a little of me in you.

After exploring in depth all the differences between the East and the West, we realized that the future is about "smashing the old clay" to make the best image of each of us. Let us focus on the similarities rather than the differences.

Let us open ourselves up, change our perspectives, be open-minded and receptive by learning from others. As the famous US philosopher Ken Wilber proposed in his Integral theory, let us "transcend and include."[2]

The Chinese have always believed that the world is a connected whole. People are not isolated and intrinsically, we are all the same. We share common aspirations of humanity and the universe. Barak Obama once said, "There is not a black America and a white America and Latino America and Asian America; there is the United States of America." Let us hope that one day, there is not a Chinese country and an American country—there is just one place that we can all call home.

---

[1] From the poem 我侬词, translated by Bruce Lee, the famous American Chinese movie star.
[2] From *A Brief History of Everything*, (Gateway, 1996, p.138).

Index

Note: Page numbers followed by "n" indicate footnotes

A

Ah Q   77–78, 78n3, 172
Alibaba   56, 56n1
All-China Federation of Industry and Commerce   55
American Born Chinese (ABC)   49
Analects of Confucius, The   10
"Apple Peel"   174
Arbitration Court of the China Chamber of International Commerce (CCOIC)   156
Art of War, The   6n1, 10, 51
Artful plagiarism   168
Atria   69

B

Baidu   157
Bayer   177
Beijing Olympic Games   48
Blink   103
Blockberry   174
Blue Ocean Strategy   14
Bo Le   8
Buddhism   15, 16, 17, 97, 167
Buffett, Warren   57, 57n2
Business banquets   132–134
  new age banquet   133
  toasts   133
BYD   56–57

C

Cao Cao   165
Chen Tonghai   64
China Central Television   173
China International Economic and Trade Arbitration Commission (CIETAC)   156
China National Offshore Oil Corporation (CNOOC)   54
China Telecom   65
China Unicom   65
China's Megatrends   14, 36
Chinese EQ   13
Chinese leaders   54–60
Circles of influence   113–125
Communist Party, The   20, 27, 31, 36, 54, 55, 65, 71, 117
Confucianism   15, 16, 17, 69, 150, 167
Confucius   10, 15, 22, 69, 80, 115, 150, 166
Confucius from the Heart: Ancient Wisdom for Today's World   69
Contracts   26, 67, 156
  dual language contract   157
Counterfeiting   169
Cultural Revolution   30, 47, 48, 54, 55, 58, 69, 74, 152, 155
  post-Cultural Revolution   47, 55
  pre-Cultural Revolution   47, 54

D

Deng Xiaoping   30, 31, 32, 40, 49, 92, 171
Dispute resolution   156–160

E

Early mover advantage   169
Economic reform   30, 32, 33, 53, 58, 70, 153

F

Family rules   151
Forbes   56, 59
Foreign-invested enterprise (FIE)   32, 52, 54, 118
Fortune   500, 64
Four ancient inventions   168
Frequent Flyer Program   120–121
Fu Chengyu   54, 55

G

Gates, Bill   11, 14, 22n2, 57, 93
General Motors   177
Generations of Chinese   47–49
Geography of Thought, The   9
Give and take   167–168
Gladwell, Malcolm   103
Global financial crisis   34, 38
Global TechCo.   1, 2
Golden Week Holiday   37
Great Leap Forward   30
Gross domestic product (GDP)   32
Gross purchasing power (GPP)   34
Guan Yuxiang   59
Guanxi   45, 102, 111, 120, 121, 123, 132, 135
Guanxi wang   21, 74

H

Haier   10
Han Chinese   171

Han Dynasty   16, 150
Hang-Tang Period   166
Hangzhou Normal College   56
Hui Chinese   171
Hukou   40
Hurun Rich List   57, 58
Hyundai Corporation   177

I

IBM   41, 177
I-Ching (Book of Changes)   17
Initial public offering (IPO)   144
Intellectual property (IP)   8, 166
   intellectual property rights (IPR)   154, 155, 178
   IP protection strategies   180
International Herald Tribune   100
iOrange   174

J

Japanese model   171
Jiang Zemin   11, 34, 93

K

Keqihua   93, 108
Key performance indicator (KPI)   14
Kuso   174

L

Lao Zi   10, 11, 15
Leadership styles   65–67
Legalism   149–150
   Legalists   149
Legend Holdings   54
Lenovo   41, 54, 55
Li Dongsheng   66, 68

Liu Chuanzhi   54, 55
Liubai   89, 92, 93

M

Ma Huateng   57
Ma, Jack   56
Mainland China   6, 12, 14, 49, 71, 127, 173
Mao Zedong   21, 27, 30, 47, 58, 177
Market capitalization   178
McDonald's   181
Mianzi   5, 10, 25–27, 45, 74, 77–78, 97–98, 111, 120, 121, 140, 144, 151
Microsoft   22, 22n2, 93, 177, 180–181
Midstream approach   144
Mobile phones   37, 43, 45, 136, 143, 144, 173, 174

N

Naisbitt, Doris   36, 36n2
Naisbitt, John   14, 36n2
Needham, Joseph   165–166, 167
New age banquet   133
New Yorker, The   173
Nikkei Business Daily   177
"No litigation" society   150–151

O

One child policy   46, 115
Open door policy   40, 172
Opening up   47, 153, 155, 156
Opium War   30

P

PetroChina   64, 178
Private-invested enterprises (PIEs)   52, 54, 65, 113

Polo, Marco   166
Providence Journal-Bulletin   9

R

Research and development (R&D)   177–178
Rushidao   17

S

Sai Weng   18, 19
Science and Civilisation in China   165
Severe Acute Respiratory Syndrome (SARS)   160
Shanghai Expo   178
Shanzhai   45–46
    Shanzai phenomenon   173, 175
Shanzhai National Spring Gala   46
Shanzhai Nobel Prize   46
Silk Market   169, 169n2, 170
Singapore   71, 171
Sinopec   64
SOE syndrome   62–63
Speed to market   42, 167
Starbucks   174, 175, 179, 180
State-owned enterprise (SOE)   31, 32, 52, 53, 62–63, 64–65, 71, 75, 75n2, 91, 92, 113, 144, 153
Sun Zi   6, 10, 51, 52

T

Tai chi talk   92, 108
Taohua   91, 92
Taoism   10, 11, 15–16, 17, 167
TCL Electronics   66, 68

Three-and-a-half localization models   170–175
Tianjin Economic-technology Development Area (TEDA)   31, 32
Time   37, 38, 42, 43, 64
Translator   103, 104, 105, 108

U

Unilever   177
Unocal   41
Unsaid message   101, 106, 108

W

Wahaha   99–101
Wall Street Journal, The   173
Wang Chuanfu   56
Wang Xisu   61
Warring States Period   150
Water Margin   173
Welch, Jack   14, 57
White talk   92–93, 108
Wholly foreign-owned enterprise (WFOE)   32, 112
Winchester, Simon   166
World factory   172, 176

World laboratory   176
World Trade Organization (WTO)   32, 153, 155

X

Xia Dynasty   149
Xiang Ma Jing   8
Xiaoping, Deng   30, 31, 32, 40, 49, 53, 92, 171, 172
Xun Zi   149, 150

Y

Yang Lan   59
Yin and yang   10, 17, 18, 43, 124, 129, 167
Yu Dan   69

Z

Zedong Mao   21, 27, 30, 31, 47, 58, 71, 74, 177
Zhang Fusen   153
Zhang Lan   58
Zhang Ruimin   10
Zhong Yong   22
Zhuang Zi   15, 29
Zhuge Liang   165, 168